HTA + VBSCRIPT + MICROSOFT.JET.OL EDB.4.0 = WORKING SMARTER AND FASTER

*Please Judge this book by its cover.
The program is inside*

Richard Edwards

STOP WISHING FOR IT

It is right here

Looking for something you or a friend of yours could use to charge up your new year with a program that works to produce results. Here it is!

This one uses Microsoft.Jet.Oledb.4.0 and the code to make it is in this book. So, what does it do?

Well, for one thing you can open all older versions of Access databases with the extension of .mdb. But they had to be created between 1998 and 2007. Otherwise, you will get an error telling you that the database was created by a newer version of Access.

Purchase the version of this product – past that time – that is in sync with the provider requirements. I have one for each version of the ACE.OLEDB provider up to Microsoft.ACE.OLEDB.15.0.

When you click the first Go button at the very top and right of the program, brings up a common dialog box:

Which I used to connect to an older database file: NWind.mdb.

Once I have done this, I click the other go button which lists all the tables and views and automates the process of creating creatable queries as seen below:

Once I decide which Query to run, because the table type, orientation and control type are set to table, Multi-Line Horizontal and span, respectively html code is generated:

```
The Code

<html>
<head>
<title>Products</title>
<style type="text/css">
body
{
    PADDING-RIGHT: 0px;
    PADDING-LEFT: 0px;
    PADDING-BOTTOM: 0px;
    MARGIN: 0px;
    COLOR: #333;
    PADDING-TOP: 0px;
    FONT-FAMILY: verdana, arial, helvetica, sans-serif;
}
table
{
    BORDER-RIGHT: #999999 3px solid;
    PADDING-RIGHT: 6px;
    PADDING-LEFT: 6px;
    FONT-WEIGHT: Bold;
    FONT-SIZE: 14px;
    PADDING-BOTTOM: 6px;
    COLOR: Peru;
    LINE-HEIGHT: 14px;
    PADDING-TOP: 6px;
    BORDER-BOTTOM: #999 1px solid;
    BACKGROUND-COLOR: #eeeeee;
    FONT-FAMILY: verdana, arial, helvetica, sans-serif;
    FONT-SIZE: 12px;
}
th
{
```

This is what the code looks like inside the program. Of course, it is a lot clearer
in the program than the image shows. At this point, clicking on View Results on the
left side of the screen:

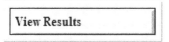

View Results

Will show you this:

ProductID	ProductName	SupplierID	CategoryID	QuantityPerUnit
1	Chai	1	1	10 boxes x 20 bags
2	Chang	1	1	24 - 12 oz bottles
3	Aniseed Syrup	1	2	12 - 550 ml bottles
4	Chef Anton	2	2	48 - 6 oz jars
5	Chef Anton	2	2	36 boxes
6	Grandma	3	2	12 - 8 oz jars
7	Uncle Bob	3	7	12 - 1 lb pkgs.
8	Northwoods Cranberry Sauce	3	2	12 - 12 oz jars
9	Mishi Kobe Niku	4	6	18 - 500 g pkgs.
10	Ikura	4	8	12 - 200 ml jars
11	Queso Cabrales	5	4	1 kg pkg.
12	Queso Manchego La Pastora	5	4	10 - 500 g pkgs.

Of course, how flashy it looks will depend on the stylesheet that you use and the additional tag that you partnered with it.

What is being offered

There is no such thing as a bugless program. Glitches happen. However, the routines – for static, dynamic, cloaked and bound have been tested and work. Additionally, the HTML ADO Coding option, pictured below, only works with the Bound coding option.

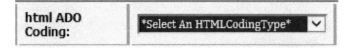

You have four basic formats:

Binding Types:	Static	☑	Dynamic	☐	Cloaked	☐	Bound	☐

Each one of these formats allows you to mix Table types: Report or table; Orientation: Multi-Line Horizontal, Multi-Line Vertical, Single-Line Horizontal and Single Line vertical; Additional Tags: Button, Combobox, Div, Listbox, Span, Textarea and Textbox; and 10 style sheets.

Meaning you have 560 ways to create Static, Dynamic, Cloaked or Bound outputs and that there are 2,240 ways you can produce html code from one database and one table.

If each only averaged 30 lines of code, those 2.240 ways to produce code would be the same outcome as one programmer could create in a year. The Products table using the Shadow Box stylesheet, came out to 1,114 lines and that took about 30 seconds to produce and display. And that is from the time the program started up to the time the view the results button was clicked on.

This program can list all the providers, drivers and ISAMS that are installed on the machine the program is running on, too.

The e-mail program is designed to be used with your Gmail account. If you don't have one, well, its probably not something you'd get any warm and fuzzies from.

If you do, the newer version of Gmail, has a switch that must be enabled in order to use it.

THE CODE NEEDED TO MAKE THIS PROGRAM WORK FOR YOU

From below the line is the code you need to create this program:

```
<html xmlns:v="urn:schemas-microsoft-com:vml">
<HEAD>
<HTA:Application
    ID = "Excalibur"
    APPLICATIONNAME = "Excalibur"
    Scroll = "no"
    SINGLEINSTANCE = "No"
    WORKSTATE = "Normal"
>
<head>
<title>Excalibur</title>
<style type='text/css'>
v\:*{ behavior: url(#default#VML);}
body
{
    PADDING-RIGHT: 0px;
    PADDING-LEFT: 0px;
    PADDING-BOTTOM: 0px;
    MARGIN: 0px;
    COLOR: #333;
```

```
      PADDING-TOP: 0px;
      FONT-FAMILY: verdana, arial, helvetica, sans-serif;
   }
   Table
   {
      BORDER-RIGHT: #999999 1px solid;
      PADDING-RIGHT: 1px;
      PADDING-LEFT: 1px;
      PADDING-BOTTOM: 1px;
      LINE-HEIGHT: 8px;
      PADDING-TOP: 1px;
      BORDER-BOTTOM: #999 1px solid;
      BACKGROUND-COLOR: #eeeeee;
      filter:progid:DXImageTransform.Microsoft.Shadow(color='silver',
Direction=135, Strength=16)
   }
   th
   {
      BORDER-RIGHT: #999999 3px solid;
      PADDING-RIGHT: 6px;
      PADDING-LEFT: 6px;
      FONT-WEIGHT: Bold;
      FONT-SIZE: 14px;
      PADDING-BOTTOM: 6px;
      COLOR: darkred;
      LINE-HEIGHT: 14px;
      PADDING-TOP: 6px;
      BORDER-BOTTOM: #999 1px solid;
      BACKGROUND-COLOR: #eeeeee;
      FONT-FAMILY: font-family: Cambria, serif;
      FONT-SIZE: 12px;
      text-align: left;
      white-Space: nowrap;
   }
   .th
   {
      BORDER-RIGHT: #999999 2px solid;
      PADDING-RIGHT: 6px;
      PADDING-LEFT: 6px;
      FONT-WEIGHT: Bold;
```

```
      PADDING-BOTTOM: 6px;
      COLOR: black;
      PADDING-TOP: 6px;
      BORDER-BOTTOM: #999 2px solid;
      BACKGROUND-COLOR: #eeeeee;
      FONT-FAMILY: font-family: Cambria, serif;
      FONT-SIZE: 10px;
      text-align: right;
      white-Space: nowrap;
}
td
{
      BORDER-RIGHT: #999999 3px solid;
      PADDING-RIGHT: 6px;
      PADDING-LEFT: 6px;
      FONT-WEIGHT: Normal;
      PADDING-BOTTOM: 6px;
      COLOR: navy;
      LINE-HEIGHT: 14px;
      PADDING-TOP: 6px;
      BORDER-BOTTOM: #999 1px solid;
      BACKGROUND-COLOR: #eeeeee;
      FONT-FAMILY: font-family: Cambria, serif;
      FONT-SIZE: 12px;
      text-align: left;
      white-Space: nowrap;
}
div
{
      BORDER-RIGHT: #999999 3px solid;
      PADDING-RIGHT: 6px;
      PADDING-LEFT: 6px;
      FONT-WEIGHT: Normal;
      PADDING-BOTTOM: 6px;
      COLOR: white;
      PADDING-TOP: 6px;
      BORDER-BOTTOM: #999 1px solid;
      BACKGROUND-COLOR: navy;
      FONT-FAMILY: font-family: Cambria, serif;
      FONT-SIZE: 10px;
```

```css
    text-align: left;
    white-Space: nowrap;
}
span
{
    BORDER-RIGHT: #999999 3px solid;
    PADDING-RIGHT: 3px;
    PADDING-LEFT: 3px;
    FONT-WEIGHT: Normal;
    PADDING-BOTTOM: 3px;
    COLOR: white;
    PADDING-TOP: 3px;
    BORDER-BOTTOM: #999 1px solid;
    BACKGROUND-COLOR: navy;
    FONT-FAMILY: font-family: Cambria, serif;
    FONT-SIZE: 10px;
    text-align: left;
    white-Space: nowrap;
    display: inline-block;
    width: 100%;
}
textarea
{
    BORDER-RIGHT: #999999 3px solid;
    PADDING-RIGHT: 3px;
    PADDING-LEFT: 3px;
    FONT-WEIGHT: Normal;
    PADDING-BOTTOM: 3px;
    COLOR: white;
    PADDING-TOP: 3px;
    BORDER-BOTTOM: #999 1px solid;
    BACKGROUND-COLOR: navy;
    FONT-FAMILY: font-family: Cambria, serif;
    FONT-SIZE: 12px;
    text-align: left;
    width: 100%;
}
select
{
    BORDER-RIGHT: #999999 1px solid;
```

```
    PADDING-RIGHT: 1px;
    PADDING-LEFT: 1px;
    FONT-WEIGHT: Normal;
    PADDING-BOTTOM: 1px;
    COLOR: white;
    PADDING-TOP: 1px;
    BORDER-BOTTOM: #999 1px solid;
    BACKGROUND-COLOR: navy;
    FONT-FAMILY: Cambria, serif;
    FONT-SIZE: 12px;
    text-align: left;
    white-Space: nowrap;
    width: 450px;
}
select1
{
    BORDER-RIGHT: #999999 1px solid;
    PADDING-RIGHT: 1px;
    PADDING-LEFT: 1px;
    FONT-WEIGHT: Normal;
    PADDING-BOTTOM: 1px;
    COLOR: white;
    PADDING-TOP: 1px;
    BORDER-BOTTOM: #999 1px solid;
    BACKGROUND-COLOR: navy;
    FONT-FAMILY: Cambria, serif;
    FONT-SIZE: 12px;
    text-align: left;
    white-Space: nowrap;
    width: 450px;
}
select2
{
    BORDER-RIGHT: #999999 1px solid;
    PADDING-RIGHT: 1px;
    PADDING-LEFT: 1px;
    FONT-WEIGHT: Normal;
    PADDING-BOTTOM: 1px;
    COLOR: white;
    PADDING-TOP: 1px;
```

```css
    BORDER-BOTTOM: #999 1px solid;
    BACKGROUND-COLOR: navy;
    FONT-FAMILY: Cambria, serif;
    FONT-SIZE: 12px;
    text-align: left;
    white-Space: nowrap;
    width: 450px;
}
#select
{
    BORDER-RIGHT: #999999 1px solid;
    PADDING-RIGHT: 1px;
    PADDING-LEFT: 1px;
    FONT-WEIGHT: Normal;
    PADDING-BOTTOM: 1px;
    COLOR: white;
    PADDING-TOP: 1px;
    BORDER-BOTTOM: #999 1px solid;
    BACKGROUND-COLOR: navy;
    FONT-FAMILY: Cambria, serif;
    FONT-SIZE: 12px;
    text-align: left;
    white-Space: nowrap;
    width: 100px;
}
select4
{
    BORDER-RIGHT: #999999 1px solid;
    PADDING-RIGHT: 1px;
    PADDING-LEFT: 1px;
    FONT-WEIGHT: Normal;
    PADDING-BOTTOM: 1px;
    COLOR: white;
    PADDING-TOP: 1px;
    BORDER-BOTTOM: #999 1px solid;
    BACKGROUND-COLOR: navy;
    FONT-FAMILY: Cambria, serif;
    FONT-SIZE: 12px;
    text-align: left;
    white-Space: nowrap;
```

```css
    width: 254px;
}
input
{
    BORDER-RIGHT: #999999 3px solid;
    PADDING-RIGHT: 3px;
    PADDING-LEFT: 3px;
    FONT-WEIGHT: Bold;
    PADDING-BOTTOM: 3px;
    COLOR: white;
    PADDING-TOP: 3px;
    BORDER-BOTTOM: #999 1px solid;
    BACKGROUND-COLOR: navy;
    FONT-FAMILY: font-family: Cambria, serif;
    FONT-SIZE: 12px;
    text-align: left;
    display: table-cell;
    white-Space: nowrap;
    width: 100%;
}
</style>
<body BGColor=#242424>
<table          style="Position:Absolute;Top:0px;Left:0px;Width:900px;Font-family:Tahoma;font-size:10px">
    <tr><th class=tdbackground align=Right Width=100px nowrap>Required Options</th>
    <th align=right style="Width:77px;" nowrap><b>Filename:</b></th>
    <td align=left nowrap><input Type='text' id='FName' name='FName' style='width:750px;'></input></td>
    <td><input          Type='Button'          id='Search'          name='Search' style='width:50px;Background-color:ButtonFace;color:black;' Value="Go!"></input></td>
    </tr>
    <tr>
    <tr><th class=tdbackground align=Right Width=115px nowrap> </th>
    <th align=right Width=77px nowrap><b>Tables: </b></th>
    <td align=left nowrap><select id="trex" style="width:125px;background-Color:navy;Color:White;"          onChange="HandlestrexChange()" name="trexPullDown"></select>
```

```
        Custom    Query: <input    Type='text'   id='CQuery'   name=CQuery'
style='width:540px;'></input>
        </td>
        <td><input Type='Button' id='LT1' name='LT1' style='width:50px;Background-
color:ButtonFace;color:black;' Value="Go!"></input></td></tr>
        </table>

        <table         style="Position:Absolute;Top:100px;Left:0px;Width:900px;Font-
family:Tahoma;font-size:10px">
        <tr><th class=tdbackground align=Center nowrap>Additional Options</th>
        <th       class="myclass"       Style="color:Black;font-family:Tahoma;font-
size:12px;width:115px;" Align=Right Nowrap>ADO Coding:</TH>
        <th><SELECT              ID="ADOCoding"              class="myclass1"
style="width:195px;background-Color:navy;Color:White"
onChange="HandlesEngineTypeChange()" name="EngineTypePullDown">
        <option Value="*Select A CodingType*">*Select A CodingType*</option>
        <option Value="cncmdrs">Connection Command And Recordset</option>
        <option Value="cnrs">Connection And Recordset</option>
        <option Value="cmdrs">Command And Recordset</option>
        <option Value="rs">Recordset</option>
        </SELECT></th>
        <th       class="myclass"       Style="color:Black;font-family:Tahoma;font-
size:12px;width:115px;" Align=Right Nowrap>html ADO Coding:</TH>
        <th><SELECT            ID="HTMLADOCoding"              class="myclass1"
style="width:195px;background-Color:navy;Color:White"
onChange="HandlesHTMLEngineTypeChange()"
name="HTMLEngineTypePullDown">
        <option     Value="*Select     An    HTMLCodingType*">*Select     An
HTMLCodingType*</option>
        <option Value="cncmdrs">Connection Command And Recordset</option>
        <option Value="cnrs">Connection And Recordset</option>
        <option Value="cmdrs">Command And Recordset</option>
        <option Value="rs">Recordset</option>
        </SELECT></th>
        <th       class="myclass"       Style="color:Black;font-family:Tahoma;font-
size:12px;width:115px;" Align=Right Nowrap>TableType:</TH>
        <th><SELECT              ID="TableType"             class="myclass1"
style="width:125px;background-Color:navy;Color:White"
onChange="HandlesTableTypeChange()" name="TableTypePullDown">
        <option Value="*Select A TableType*">*Select An Option*</option>
```

```
<option Value="Table">Table</option>
<option Value="Report">Report</option>
</SELECT></th>
</tr>
<tr>
<th class=tdbackground align=Center nowrap> </th><th class="myclass"
Style="color:Black;font-family:Tahoma;font-size:12px"    Align=Right    nowrap>
Orientation:</TH>
<th>
<SELECT         class="myclass1"         style="width:125px;background-
Color:navy;Color:White"              onChange="HandlesOrientationChange()"
name="OrientationPullDown">
<option selected Value="*Select An Orientation*">*Select An Option*</option>
<option Value="Multi-Line Horizontal">Multi-Line Horizontal</option>
<option Value="Multi-Line Vertical">Multi-Line Vertical</option>
<option Value="Single-Line Horizontal">Single-Line Horizontal</option>
<option Value="Single-Line Vertical">Single-Line Vertical</option>
</SELECT></TH>
<TH   class="myclass"   Style="color:Black;font-family:Tahoma;font-size:12px"
Align=Right nowrap>    Additional Tags:</TH>
<TH>
<SELECT         class="myclass1"         style="width:125px;background-
Color:navy;Color:White"              onChange="HandlesControlTypeChange()"
name="ControlTypePullDown">
<option    selected    Value="*Select    An    Additional    Tag*">*Select    An
Option*</option>
<option Value="Button">Button</option>
<option Value="Combobox">Combobox</option>
<option Value="Div">Div</option>
<option Value="Listbox">Listbox</option>
<option Value="Span">Span</option>
<option Value="Textarea">Textarea</option>
<option Value="Textbox">Textbox</option>
</SELECT></TH>
<TH   class="myclass"   Style="color:Black;font-family:Tahoma;font-size:12px"
Align=Right nowrap>    StyleSheets:</TH>
<TH>
<SELECT         class="myclass"         style="width:125px;background-
Color:navy;Color:White"              onChange="HandlesStyleSheetChange()"
name="StyleSheetPullDown">
```

```html
<option selected Value="*Select A StyleSheet*">*Select An Option*</option>
<option Value="None">None</option>
<option Value="Basic">Basic</option>
<option Value="InLine">InLine</option>
<option Value="BlackAndWhiteText">Black And White Text</option>
<option Value="OscillatingRowColors">Oscillating Row Colors</option>
<option Value="ColoredText">Colored Text</option>
<option Value="GhostDecorated">Ghost Decorated</Option>
<option Value="3D">3d</option>
<option Value="ShadowBox">Shadow Box</option>
<option Value="Customized">Customized</options>
</select></TH></TR>
</table>
<table            style="Position:Absolute;Top:190px;Left:0px;Width:400px;Font-family:Tahoma;font-size:10px">
<tr><th                    class="myclass"                    Style="background-Color:buttonface;color:darkred;font-family:Tahoma;font-size:12px;Width:115px" Align=Right nowrap>Binding Types:</th>
<th   Style="background-Color:buttonface;color:Black;font-family:Tahoma;font-size:12px" Align=Right nowrap>Static</th>
<th><input      type='checkbox'      id='st'      name='st'      checked=true style="width:25px;background-Color:buttonface;Color:black"></input></th>
<th   Style="background-Color:buttonface;color:Black;font-family:Tahoma;font-size:12px" Align=Right nowrap>Dynamic</th>
<th><input        type='checkbox'        id='dynamic'        name='dynamic' style="width:25px;background-Color:buttonface;Color:black"></input></th>
<th   Style="background-Color:buttonface;color:Black;font-family:Tahoma;font-size:12px" Align=Right nowrap>Cloaked</th>
<th><input        type='checkbox'        id='cloaked'        name='cloaked' style="width:25px;background-Color:buttonface;Color:black"></input></th>
<th   Style="background-Color:buttonface;color:Black;font-family:Tahoma;font-size:12px" Align=Right nowrap>Bound</th>
<th><input        type='checkbox'        id='bound'        name='bound' style="width:25px;background-Color:buttonface;Color:black"></input></th>
</tr>
</table>
<table   style="Position:Absolute;Top:245px;Left:0px;Font-family:Tahoma;font-size:10px">
<TR><TH      class=td      background      align=Center      nowrap colspan=6>Checks</TH></TR>
```

```
<TR>
<TH align=left nowrap>
<input          Type='Button'          id='Providers'          name='Providers'
style='width:150px;Background-color:ButtonFace;color:black;'          Value="List
Providers"></input>
</TH></TR>
<TR>
<TH align=left nowrap>
<input          Type='Button'          id='ISAMS'          name='ISAMS'
style='width:150px;Background-color:ButtonFace;color:black;' Value="List Installed
ISAMS"></input>
</TH></TR>
<TR>
<TH align=left nowrap">
<input          Type='Button'          id='Drivers'          name='Drivers'
style='width:150px;Background-color:ButtonFace;color:black;' Value="List Installed
Drivers"></input>
</th></tr>
<TR>
<TH align=left nowrap>
<input          Type='Button'          id='DataLinks1'          name='DataLinks1'
style='width:150px;Background-color:ButtonFace;color:black;'          Value="Use
Connection Helper"></input>
</TH></TR>
<TR>
<TH align=left nowrap">
<input          Type='Button'          id='Createtemplate'          name='CreateTemplate'
style='width:150px;Background-color:ButtonFace;color:black;'          Value="Create
Template"></input>
</TH></TR>
<TH align=left nowrap>
<input          Type='Button'          id='UseTemplate'          name='UseTemplate'
style='width:150px;Background-color:ButtonFace;color:black;'          Value="Use
Template"></input>
</TH></TR>
<TR><TH          class=td          background          align=Center          nowrap
colspan=5>Actions</TH></TR>
<TR>
<TH align=left nowrap>
```

```
    <input        Type='Button'        id='Clipboard1'        name='Clipboard1'
style='width:150px;Background-color:ButtonFace;color:black;'    Value="Copy    To
Clipboard"></input>
    </TH>
    </TR>
    <TR>
    <TH align=left nowrap>
    <input        Type='Button'        id='RunMe'        name='RunMe'
style='width:150px;Background-color:ButtonFace;color:black;'        Value="Run
Code"></input>
    </TH></TR>
    <TR>
    <TH align=left nowrap>
    <input        Type='Button'        id='ViewMe'        name='ViewMe'
style='width:150px;Background-color:ButtonFace;color:black;'        Value="View
Results"></input>
    </TH></TR>
    <TR>
    <TH align=left nowrap>
    <input        Type='Button'        id='Document'        name='Documenter'
style='width:150px;Background-color:ButtonFace;color:black;'        Value="Use
Documented Code"></input>
    </TH></TR>

    <TR><TH    align=left    nowrap><input    Type='Button'    id='wd'    name='wd'
style='width:150px;Background-color:ButtonFace;color:black;'    Value="Create    Word
Document"></input></TH></TR>

    <TR>
    <TH align=left nowrap>
    <input        Type='Button'        id='EMAIL'        name='EMAIL'
style='width:150px;Background-color:ButtonFace;color:black;'        Value="E-Mail
Results"></input>
    </TH></TR>
    </table>
    </table>

    <TABLE                style="Position:Absolute;Top:245px;Left:180px;Font-
family:Tahoma;font-size:10px">
    <TR><TH>
```

```
    <v:roundrect id="A" style="width:120;height:30px" arcsize="5%">
    <v:fill    color="#CCCCCC"    color2="white"    Opacity=90%    Opacity2=90%
method="linear sigma" angle="-135" type="gradientradial" />
    <v:textbox         id="A1"         style="font-family:Garmond;Font-
size:12px;Color:darkred"><b>The Code</b></v:textbox>
    <v:shadow    id="A2"    on="false"    offset="3pt,    3pt"    opacity="70%"
color="black"/>
    </v:roundrect>
  </TH></TR>
  </TABLE>
  <TABLE                            style="border:solid;border-color:Blue;border-
width:1px;Position:Absolute;Left:180;Top:285px;width:832px;Height:505px">
  <TR><TH><Textarea    ID="Textarea1"    name="Textarea1"    Style="font-
family:Courier                                New;Height:505px;Width:832px;"
wrap="off"></textarea></TH></TR>
  </TABLE>


  <Table      class="myclass"      Style="border:outset;border-color:Silver;border-
width:1px;position:absolute;top:820px;left:0px;">
  <tr><th class=tdbackground align=Center nowrap colspan=10>Required E-MAIL
Properties</th></tr>
  <TR><TH       class="myclass"       Style="color:Black;font-family:Tahoma;font-
size:10px" Align=Right Nowrap>ServerName:</TH>
  <th>
  <Input        type='text'        id=sn        style="width:150px;background-
Color:navy;Color:White"></input>
  </th>
  <th    class="myclass"    Style="color:Black;font-family:Tahoma;font-size:10px"
Align=Right nowrap>LoginUser:</TH>
  <th>
  <Input        type='text'        id=lnu        style="width:150px;background-
Color:navy;Color:White"></input>
  </TH>
  <TH    class="myclass"    Style="color:Black;font-family:Tahoma;font-size:10px"
Align=Right nowrap>Password:</TH>
  <TH>
  <Input        type='password'        id=lpwd        style="width:150px;background-
Color:navy;Color:White"></input>
  </TH>
```

```
<TH   class="myclass"   Style="color:Black;font-family:Tahoma;font-size:10px"
Align=Right nowrap>Your Mail Name:</TH>
   <TH>
   <Input        type='text'        id=emfn        style="width:150px;background-
Color:navy;Color:White"></input>
   </TH>
   </TR>
   <TR><TH   class="myclass"   Style="color:Black;font-family:Tahoma;font-
size:10px" Align=Right Nowrap>Your Mail Address:</TH>
   <th>
   <Input        type='text'        id=ema        style="width:150px;background-
Color:navy;Color:White"></input>
   </th>
   <th   class="myclass"   Style="color:Black;font-family:Tahoma;font-size:10px"
Align=Right nowrap>Sending it to:</TH>
   <th>
   <Input        type='text'        id="rec"        style="width:150px;background-
Color:navy;Color:White"></input>
   </TH>
   <TH   class="myclass"   Style="color:Black;font-family:Tahoma;font-size:10px"
Align=Right nowrap>Subject</TH>
   <TH colspan=4>
   <Input        type='text'        id=s        style="width:415px;background-
Color:navy;Color:White"></input>
   </TH>
   </TR>
   </table>


   <script language="vbscript">

   Dim cnstr
   Dim cn
   Dim Provider
   Dim rs

   Dim EngineConfiguration
   Dim HTMLEngineConfiguration
   Dim txtstream
   Dim TableType
```

```
Dim Orientation
Dim ControlType
Dim Filename
Dim strQuery
Dim Tablename
Dim Value
Dim StyleSheet


Provider="Microsoft.Jet.OleDb.4.0"

Filename = ""
strQuery = ""
Tablename = ""

EngineConfiguration = "rs"
HTMLEngineConfiguration = "rs"
TableType = "Table"
Orientation = "Multi-Line Horizontal"
ControlType = "Span"
StyleSheet = "InLine"

Sub Window_onLoad()

    window.moveTo 0, 0
    window.resizeTo 1055, 975
    RunMe.Disabled = true

End Sub

Sub HandlesEngineTypeChange()

    If EngineTypePullDown.Value <> "*Select An Option*" then

        EngineConfiguration = EngineTypePullDown.Value

    End If

End sub
```

```
Sub HandlesHTMLEngineTypeChange()

    If HTMLEngineTypePullDown.Value <> "*Select An Option*" then

        HTMLEngineConfiguration = HTMLEngineTypePullDown.Value

    End If

End sub

Sub st_OnClick()
  If st.Checked = true then
    dynamic.Checked = false
    cloaked.Checked = false
    bound.Checked = false
    If trexPullDown.Value <> "*Select An Option*" then
       Write_The_Code
    End If
  End If
End Sub

Sub dynamic_OnClick()
  If dynamic.Checked = true then
    st.Checked = false
    cloaked.Checked = false
    bound.Checked = false
    If trexPullDown.Value <> "*Select An Option*" then
       Write_The_Code
    End If
  End If
End Sub

Sub cloaked_OnClick()
  If cloaked.Checked = true then
    dynamic.Checked = false
    st.Checked = false
    bound.Checked = false
    If trexPullDown.Value <> "*Select An Option*" then
       Write_The_Code
    End If
```

```
      End If
   End Sub

   Sub bound_OnClick()
      If bound.Checked = true then
         dynamic.Checked = false
         cloaked.Checked = false
         st.Checked = false
         If trexPullDown.Value <> "*Select An Option*" then
            Write_The_Code
         End If
      End If
   End Sub


   Sub HandlesTableTypeChange()

      If TableTypePullDown.Value <> "*Select A TableType*" Then
         TableType = TableTypePullDown.Value
         Write_The_Code

      End If

   End Sub


   Sub HandlestrexChange()

      If trexPullDown.Value <> "*Select An Option*" then

         dim pos
         pos = instr(trexPullDown.Value, " ")
         if pos > 0 then
            CQuery.Value = "Select * From [" & trexPullDown.Value & "]"
         else
            CQuery.Value = "Select * From " & trexPullDown.Value
         End If

      End If
```

```
End Sub


Sub HandlesOrientationChange()

  If OrientationPullDown.Value <> "*Select An Orientation*" Then
    Orientation = OrientationPullDown.Value
    Write_The_Code
  End If

End Sub

Sub HandlesControlTypeChange()

  If ControlTypePullDown.Value <> "*Select An Additional Tag*" Then
    ControlType = ControlTypePullDown.Value
    Write_The_Code
  End If

End Sub

Sub HandlesStyleSheetChange()

If StyleSheetPullDown.Value <> "*Select A StyleSheet*" Then
    StyleSheet = StyleSheetPullDown.Value
    Write_The_Code
End If

End Sub

Sub Write_The_Code()

    textarea1.innerText = ""

    If FName.Value = "" then
        msgbox("Please provide the location and name of the database you want
to use before clicking here.")
        exit sub
    else
        Filename = FName.Value
```

```
End If

If CQuery.Value = "" then
    msgbox("Please create a Query string before clicking here.")
    exit sub
End If

strQuery = CQuery.Value

dim pos
pos = instr(trexPullDown.Value, " ")
if pos > 0 then
    Tablename = Replace(trexPullDown.Value, " ", "_")
else
    Tablename = trexPullDown.Value
End If

if st.Checked = True then
    Do_Static
    Exit Sub

End If

if dynamic.Checked = True then

    Do_Dynamic
    Exit Sub

End If

if cloaked.Checked = True then

    Do_Cloaked
    Exit Sub

End If

if bound.Checked = True then

    Do_Bound
```

```
        Exit Sub

    End If

End sub


Sub Do_Static()

  Select Case EngineConfiguration


    Case "cncmdrs"


          Set cn = CreateObject("ADODB.Connection")
          Set cmd = CreateObject("ADODB.Command")
          Set rs = CreateObject("ADODB.Recordset")


          cn.ConnectionString = "Provider=" & Provider & ";Data Source=" &
fName.Value & ";"
          Call cn.Open()

          cmd.ActiveConnection = cn
          cmd.CommandType = 8
          cmd.CommandText = strQuery
          Call cmd.Execute()

          rs.CursorLocation = 3
          rs.LockType = 3
          Call rs.Open(cmd)


      Case "cnrs"


          Set cn = CreateObject("ADODB.Connection")
          Set rs = CreateObject("ADODB.Recordset")
```

```vb
            cn.ConnectionString = "Provider=" & Provider & ";Data Source=" &
fName.Value & ";"
            Call cn.Open()

            rs.ActiveConnection = cn
            rs.CursorLocation = 3
            rs.LockType = 3
            rs.Source = strQuery
            Call rs.Open()

      Case "cmdrs"

            Set cmd = CreateObject("ADODB.Command")
            Set rs = CreateObject("ADODB.Recordset")

            cmd.ActiveConnection = "Provider=" & Provider & ";Data Source=" &
fName.Value & ";"
            cmd.CommandType = 8
            cmd.CommandText = strQuery
            Call cmd.Execute()

            rs.CursorLocation = 3
            rs.LockType = 3
            Call rs.Open(cmd)

      Case "rs"

         Set rs = CreateObject("ADODB.Recordset")
         rs.ActiveConnection = "Provider=" & Provider & ";Data Source=" &
fName.Value & ";"
            rs.LockType = 3
            rs.Cursorlocation = 3
            rs.Source = strQuery
            Call rs.Open()

      End Select


      Set ws = CreateObject("WScript.Shell")
```

```
        Set fso = CreateObject("Scripting.FileSystemObject")

        Set txtstream = fso.OpenTextFile(ws.CurrentDirectory & "\" & tablename &
".html", 2, True, -2)
        txtstream.WriteLine("<html>")
        txtstream.WriteLine("<head>")
        txtstream.WriteLine("<title>" & Tablename & "</title>")

    Add_The_StyleSheet

        txtstream.WriteLine("</head>")
        txtstream.WriteLine("<body>")
        txtstream.WriteLine("")

        If StyleSheet = "InLine" Then


        Select Case Orientation


            Case "Single-Line Horizontal"

                Select Case TableType

                    Case "Table"

                        txtstream.WriteLine("<table       Border='1'       cellpadding='1'
cellspacing='1' datasrc=#rs>")

                    Case "Report"

                        txtstream.WriteLine("<table       Border='0'       cellpadding='1'
cellspacing='1' datasrc=#rs>")

                End Select


                txtstream.WriteLine("<tr>")
                For x = 0 To rs.Fields.Count - 1
```

```
        txtstream.WriteLine("<th        style='font-family:Calibri,        Sans-
Serif;font-size: 12px;color:darkred;'>" & rs.Fields(x).Name & "</th>")


            Next
            txtstream.WriteLine("</tr>")
            txtstream.WriteLine("<tr>")
            For x = 0 To rs.Fields.Count - 1


                Select Case ControlType


                    Case "None"
                            txtstream.WriteLine("<td                style='font-
family:Calibri,  Sans-Serif;font-size:  12px;color:navy;'>"  &  rs.Fields(x).Value  &
"</td>")
                    Case "Button"
                            txtstream.WriteLine("<td                style='font-
family:Calibri, Sans-Serif;font-size: 12px;color:navy;'><input type=button Value='"
& rs.Fields(x).Value & "'></input></td>")
                    Case "Combobox"
                            txtstream.WriteLine("<td                style='font-
family:Calibri, Sans-Serif;font-size: 12px;color:navy;'><select><option Value='" &
rs.Fields(x).Value & "'>" & rs.Fields(x).Value & "</option></select></td>")
                    Case "Div"
                            txtstream.WriteLine("<td                style='font-
family:Calibri, Sans-Serif;font-size: 12px;color:navy;'><div>" & rs.Fields(x).Value &
"</div></td>")
                    Case "Listbox"
                            txtstream.WriteLine("<td                style='font-
family:Calibri,            Sans-Serif;font-size:            12px;color:navy;'><select
multiple=true><option Value ='" & rs.Fields(x).Value & "'>" & rs.Fields(x).Value &
"</option></select></td>")
                    Case "Span"
                            txtstream.WriteLine("<td                style='font-
family:Calibri, Sans-Serif;font-size: 12px;color:navy;'><span>" & rs.Fields(x).Value
& "</span></td>")
                    Case "Textbox"
                            txtstream.WriteLine("<td                style='font-
family:Calibri, Sans-Serif;font-size: 12px;color:navy;'><input type=text Value='" &
rs.Fields(x).Value & "'></input></td>")
```

```
            Case "Textarea"
                    txtstream.WriteLine("<td              style='font-
family:Calibri,      Sans-Serif;font-size:     12px;color:navy;'><textarea>"      &
rs.Fields(x).Value & "</textarea></td>")

            End Select


        Next

        txtstream.WriteLine("</tr>")


    Case "Multi-Line Horizontal"

    Select Case TableType

        Case "Table"

            txtstream.WriteLine("<table      Border='1'     cellpadding='1'
cellspacing='1'>")

        Case "Report"

            txtstream.WriteLine("<table      Border='0'     cellpadding='1'
cellspacing='1'>")

    End Select

    txtstream.WriteLine("<tr>")
    For x = 0 To rs.Fields.Count - 1

            txtstream.WriteLine("<th     style='font-family:Calibri,     Sans-
Serif;font-size: 12px;color:darkred;'>" & rs.Fields(x).Name & "</th>")

        Next
    txtstream.WriteLine("</tr>")
    Do While rs.EOF = False
```

```
txtstream.WriteLine("<tr>")
For x = 0 To rs.Fields.Count - 1

    Select Case ControlType

        Case "None"
                            txtstream.WriteLine("<td    style='font-
family:Calibri, Sans-Serif;font-size: 12px;color:navy;'>" & rs.Fields(x).Value &
"</td>")
        Case "Button"
                            txtstream.WriteLine("<td    style='font-
family:Calibri, Sans-Serif;font-size: 12px;color:navy;'><input type=button Value='"
& rs.Fields(x).Value & "'></input></td>")
        Case "Combobox"
                            txtstream.WriteLine("<td    style='font-
family:Calibri, Sans-Serif;font-size: 12px;color:navy;'><select><option Value='" &
rs.Fields(x).Value & "'>" & rs.Fields(x).Value & "</option></select></td>")
        Case "Div"
                            txtstream.WriteLine("<td    style='font-
family:Calibri, Sans-Serif;font-size: 12px;color:navy;'><div>" & rs.Fields(x).Value &
"</div></td>")
        Case "Listbox"
                            txtstream.WriteLine("<td    style='font-
family:Calibri,          Sans-Serif;font-size:          12px;color:navy;'><select
multiple=true><option Value ='" & rs.Fields(x).Value & "'>" & rs.Fields(x).Value &
"</option></select></td>")
        Case "Span"
                            txtstream.WriteLine("<td    style='font-
family:Calibri, Sans-Serif;font-size: 12px;color:navy;'><span>" & rs.Fields(x).Value
& "</span></td>")
        Case "Textbox"
                            txtstream.WriteLine("<td    style='font-
family:Calibri, Sans-Serif;font-size: 12px;color:navy;'><input type=text Value='" &
rs.Fields(x).Value & "'></input></td>")
        Case "Textarea"
                            txtstream.WriteLine("<td    style='font-
family:Calibri,          Sans-Serif;font-size:          12px;color:navy;'><textarea>"          &
rs.Fields(x).Value & "</textarea></td>")
```

```
                End Select


            Next
            txtstream.WriteLine("</tr>")
            rs.MoveNext()
        Loop



        Case "Single-Line Vertical"


            Select Case TableType

                Case "Table"

                    txtstream.WriteLine("<table       Border='1'       cellpadding='1'
cellspacing='1'>")

                    Case "Report"

                    txtstream.WriteLine("<table       Border='0'       cellpadding='1'
cellspacing='1'>")

                End Select

            For x = 0 To rs.Fields.Count - 1

                Select Case ControlType

                    Case "None"
                                txtstream.WriteLine("<tr><th         style='font-
family:Calibri, Sans-Serif;font-size: 12px;color:darkred;'>" & rs.Fields(x).Name &
"</th><td  style='font-family:Calibri, Sans-Serif;font-size: 12px;color:navy;'>" &
rs.Fields(x).Value & "</td></tr>")
                    Case "Button"
                                txtstream.WriteLine("<tr><th         style='font-
family:Calibri, Sans-Serif;font-size: 12px;color:darkred;'>" & rs.Fields(x).Name &
```

```
"</th><td style='font-family:Calibri, Sans-Serif;font-size: 12px;color:navy;'><input
type=button Value='" & rs.Fields(x).Value & "'></input></td></tr>")
                Case "Combobox"

                        txtstream.WriteLine("<tr><th        style='font-
family:Calibri, Sans-Serif;font-size: 12px;color:darkred;'>" & rs.Fields(x).Name &
"</th>        <td        style='font-family:Calibri,        Sans-Serif;font-size:
12px;color:navy;'><select><option    Value='"    &    rs.Fields(x).Value    &    "'>"    &
rs.Fields(x).Value & "</option></select></td></tr>")
                Case "Div"

                        txtstream.WriteLine("<tr><th        style='font-
family:Calibri, Sans-Serif;font-size: 12px;color:darkred;'>" & rs.Fields(x).Name &
"</th><td style='font-family:Calibri, Sans-Serif;font-size: 12px;color:navy;'><div>"
& rs.Fields(x).Value & "</div></td></tr>")
                Case "Listbox"

                        txtstream.WriteLine("<tr><th        style='font-
family:Calibri, Sans-Serif;font-size: 12px;color:darkred;'>" & rs.Fields(x).Name &
"</th><td style='font-family:Calibri, Sans-Serif;font-size: 12px;color:navy;'><select
multiple=true><option Value ='" & rs.Fields(x).Value & "'>" & rs.Fields(x).Value &
"</option></select></td></tr>")
                Case "Span"

                        txtstream.WriteLine("<tr><th        style='font-
family:Calibri, Sans-Serif;font-size: 12px;color:darkred;'>" & rs.Fields(x).Name &
"</th><td        style='font-family:Calibri,        Sans-Serif;font-size:
12px;color:navy;'><span>" & rs.Fields(x).Value & "</span></td></tr>")
                Case "Textbox"

                        txtstream.WriteLine("<tr><th        style='font-
family:Calibri, Sans-Serif;font-size: 12px;color:darkred;'>" & rs.Fields(x).Name &
"</th><td style='font-family:Calibri, Sans-Serif;font-size: 12px;color:navy;'><input
type=text Value='" & rs.Fields(x).Value & "'></input></td></tr>")
                Case "Textarea"

                        txtstream.WriteLine("<tr><th        style='font-
family:Calibri, Sans-Serif;font-size: 12px;color:darkred;'>" & rs.Fields(x).Name &
"</th><td        style='font-family:Calibri,        Sans-Serif;font-size:
12px;color:navy;'><textarea>" & rs.Fields(x).Value & "</textarea></td></tr>")


        End Select

    Next
```

Case "Multi-Line Vertical"

Select Case TableType

Case "Table"

txtstream.WriteLine("<table   Border='1'   cellpadding='1' cellspacing='1'>")

Case "Report"

txtstream.WriteLine("<table   Border='0'   cellpadding='1' cellspacing='1'>")

End Select

For x = 0 To rs.Fields.Count - 1

txtstream.WriteLine("<tr><th   style='font-family:Calibri,   Sans-Serif;font-size: 12px;color:darkred;'>" & rs.Fields(x).Name & "</th>")

rs.MoveFirst()

Do While rs.EOF = False

Select Case ControlType

Case "None"
txtstream.WriteLine("<td   style='font-family:Calibri,   Sans-Serif;font-size: 12px;color:navy;'>" & rs.Fields(x).Value & "</td>")
Case "Button"
txtstream.WriteLine("<td   style='font-family:Calibri, Sans-Serif;font-size: 12px;color:navy;'><input type=button Value='" & rs.Fields(x).Value & "'></input></td>")
Case "Combobox"

```
                            txtstream.WriteLine("<td    style='font-
family:Calibri, Sans-Serif;font-size: 12px;color:navy;'><select><option Value='" &
rs.Fields(x).Value & "'>" & rs.Fields(x).Value & "</option></select></td>")
                Case "Div"
                            txtstream.WriteLine("<td    style='font-
family:Calibri, Sans-Serif;font-size: 12px;color:navy;'><div>" & rs.Fields(x).Value &
"</div></td>")
                Case "Listbox"
                            txtstream.WriteLine("<td    style='font-
family:Calibri,        Sans-Serif;font-size:        12px;color:navy;'><select
multiple=true><option Value ='" & rs.Fields(x).Value & "'>" & rs.Fields(x).Value &
"</option></select></td>")
                Case "Span"
                            txtstream.WriteLine("<td    style='font-
family:Calibri, Sans-Serif;font-size: 12px;color:navy;'><span>" & rs.Fields(x).Value
& "</span></td>")
                Case "Textbox"
                            txtstream.WriteLine("<td    style='font-
family:Calibri, Sans-Serif;font-size: 12px;color:navy;'><input type=text Value='" &
rs.Fields(x).Value & "'></input></td>")
                Case "Textarea"
                            txtstream.WriteLine("<td    style='font-
family:Calibri,    Sans-Serif;font-size:    12px;color:navy;'><textarea>"    &
rs.Fields(x).Value & "</textarea></td>")


        End Select

        rs.MoveNext()

    Loop

    txtstream.WriteLine("</tr>")

  Next


  End Select
```

```
Else

    Select Case Orientation

        Case "Single-Line Horizontal"

        Select Case TableType

            Case "Table"

                txtstream.WriteLine("<table          Border='1'       cellpadding='1'
cellspacing='1' datasrc=#rs>")

                Case "Report"

                txtstream.WriteLine("<table          Border='0'       cellpadding='1'
cellspacing='1' datasrc=#rs>")

            End Select


            txtstream.WriteLine("<tr>")
            For x = 0 To rs.Fields.Count - 1

                txtstream.WriteLine("<th>" & rs.Fields(x).Name & "</th>")

            Next
            txtstream.WriteLine("</tr>")
            txtstream.WriteLine("<tr>")
            For x = 0 To rs.Fields.Count - 1


            Select Case ControlType

                Case "None"
                            txtstream.WriteLine("<td>" &  rs.Fields(x).Value
& "</td>")
                Case "Button"
```

```vb
                                txtstream.WriteLine("<td><input    type=button
Value='" & rs.Fields(x).Value & "'></input></td>")
                Case "Combobox"
                                txtstream.WriteLine("<td><select><option
Value='"    &    rs.Fields(x).Value    &    "'>"    &    rs.Fields(x).Value    &
"</option></select></td>")
                Case "Div"
                                txtstream.WriteLine("<td><div>"              &
rs.Fields(x).Value & "</div></td>")
                Case "Listbox"
                                txtstream.WriteLine("<td><select
multiple=true><option Value ='" & rs.Fields(x).Value & "'>" & rs.Fields(x).Value &
"</option></select></td>")
                Case "Span"
                                txtstream.WriteLine("<td><span>"             &
rs.Fields(x).Value & "</span></td>")
                Case "Textbox"
                                txtstream.WriteLine("<td><input       type=text
Value='" & rs.Fields(x).Value & "'></input></td>")
                Case "Textarea"
                                txtstream.WriteLine("<td><textarea>"          &
rs.Fields(x).Value & "</textarea></td>")

            End Select


            Next

            txtstream.WriteLine("</tr>")


        Case "Multi-Line Horizontal"


            Select Case TableType

            Case "Table"
```

```
                    txtstream.WriteLine("<table      Border='1'      cellpadding='1'
cellspacing='1'>")

            Case "Report"

                    txtstream.WriteLine("<table      Border='0'      cellpadding='1'
cellspacing='1'>")

        End Select

        txtstream.WriteLine("<tr>")
        For x = 0 To rs.Fields.Count - 1

            txtstream.WriteLine("<th>" & rs.Fields(x).Name & "</th>")

        Next
        txtstream.WriteLine("</tr>")
        Do While rs.EOF = False

            txtstream.WriteLine("<tr>")
            For x = 0 To rs.Fields.Count - 1

                Select Case ControlType

                    Case "None"
                                        txtstream.WriteLine("<td>"             &
rs.Fields(x).Value & "</td>")
                    Case "Button"
                                        txtstream.WriteLine("<td><input
type=button Value='" & rs.Fields(x).Value & "'></input></td>")
                    Case "Combobox"

            txtstream.WriteLine("<td><select><option Value='" & rs.Fields(x).Value &
"'>" & rs.Fields(x).Value & "</option></select></td>")
                    Case "Div"
                                        txtstream.WriteLine("<td><div>"        &
rs.Fields(x).Value & "</div></td>")
                    Case "Listbox"
```

```
                                        txtstream.WriteLine("<td><select
multiple=true><option Value ='" & rs.Fields(x).Value & "'>" & rs.Fields(x).Value &
"</option></select></td>")
                        Case "Span"
                                        txtstream.WriteLine("<td><span>"    &
rs.Fields(x).Value & "</span></td>")
                        Case "Textbox"
                                                txtstream.WriteLine("<td><input
type=text Value='" & rs.Fields(x).Value & "'></input></td>")
                        Case "Textarea"
                                        txtstream.WriteLine("<td><textarea>"
& rs.Fields(x).Value & "</textarea></td>")

                End Select


            Next
            txtstream.WriteLine("</tr>")
            rs.MoveNext()
        Loop



        Case "Single-Line Vertical"


        Select Case TableType

        Case "Table"

                txtstream.WriteLine("<table       Border='1'      cellpadding='1'
cellspacing='1'>")

                Case "Report"

                txtstream.WriteLine("<table       Border='0'      cellpadding='1'
cellspacing='1'>")

                End Select
```

```
For x = 0 To rs.Fields.Count - 1

    Select Case ControlType

        Case "None"
                    txtstream.WriteLine("<tr><th>"                    &
rs.Fields(x).Name & "</th><td>" & rs.Fields(x).Value & "</td></tr>")
        Case "Button"
                    txtstream.WriteLine("<tr><th>"                    &
rs.Fields(x).Name & "</th><td><input type=button Value='" & rs.Fields(x).Value &
"'></input></td></tr>")
        Case "Combobox"
                    txtstream.WriteLine("<tr><th>"                    &
rs.Fields(x).Name & "</th> <td><select><option Value='" & rs.Fields(x).Value &
"'>" & rs.Fields(x).Value & "</option></select></td></tr>")
        Case "Div"
                    txtstream.WriteLine("<tr><th>"                    &
rs.Fields(x).Name & "</th><td><div>" & rs.Fields(x).Value & "</div></td></tr>")
        Case "Listbox"
                    txtstream.WriteLine("<tr><th>"                    &
rs.Fields(x).Name  &  "</th><td><select  multiple=true><option  Value ='"  &
rs.Fields(x).Value & "'>" & rs.Fields(x).Value & "</option></select></td></tr>")
        Case "Span"
                    txtstream.WriteLine("<tr><th>"                    &
rs.Fields(x).Name    &    "</th><td><span>"    &    rs.Fields(x).Value    &
"</span></td></tr>")
        Case "Textbox"
                    txtstream.WriteLine("<tr><th>"                    &
rs.Fields(x).Name & "</th><td><input type=text Value='" & rs.Fields(x).Value &
"'></input></td></tr>")
        Case "Textarea"
                    txtstream.WriteLine("<tr><th>"                    &
rs.Fields(x).Name    &    "</th><td><textarea>"    &    rs.Fields(x).Value    &
"</textarea></td></tr>")

    End Select

Next
```

```
Case "Multi-Line Vertical"

    Select Case TableType

        Case "Table"

            txtstream.WriteLine("<table    Border='1'    cellpadding='1'
cellspacing='1'>")

        Case "Report"

            txtstream.WriteLine("<table    Border='0'    cellpadding='1'
cellspacing='1'>")

    End Select


    For x = 0 To rs.Fields.Count - 1

        txtstream.WriteLine("<tr><th>" & rs.Fields(x).Name & "</th>")

        rs.MoveFirst()

        Do While rs.EOF = False


            Select Case ControlType

                Case "None"
                                txtstream.WriteLine("<td>"            &
rs.Fields(x).Value & "</td>")
                Case "Button"
                                txtstream.WriteLine("<td><input
type=button Value='" & rs.Fields(x).Value & "'></input></td>")
                Case "Combobox"

        txtstream.WriteLine("<td><select><option Value='" & rs.Fields(x).Value &
"'>" & rs.Fields(x).Value & "</option></select></td>")
                Case "Div"
```

```
                                        txtstream.WriteLine("<td><div>"      &
rs.Fields(x).Value & "</div></td>")
                    Case "Listbox"
                                        txtstream.WriteLine("<td><select
multiple=true><option Value ='" & rs.Fields(x).Value & "'>" & rs.Fields(x).Value &
"</option></select></td>")
                    Case "Span"
                                        txtstream.WriteLine("<td><span>"      &
rs.Fields(x).Value & "</span></td>")
                    Case "Textbox"
                                        txtstream.WriteLine("<td><input
type=text Value='" & rs.Fields(x).Value & "'></input></td>")
                    Case "Textarea"
                                        txtstream.WriteLine("<td><textarea>"
& rs.Fields(x).Value & "</textarea></td>")

            End Select

            rs.MoveNext()

        Loop

        txtstream.WriteLine("</tr>")

    Next


    End Select


End If

txtstream.WriteLine("</table>")
txtstream.WriteLine("</body>")
txtstream.WriteLine("</html>")
txtstream.Close
```

```
            tempstr = ""
            Set txtstream = fso.OpenTextFile(ws.CurrentDirectory & "\" & Tablename &
".html", 1, true, -2)
            Do While txtstream.AtEndOfStream = false
               tempstr = tempstr & txtstream.ReadLine()
               tempstr = tempstr & vbcrlf
            loop
            txtstream.Close
            textarea1.innerText = tempstr


      End Sub

      Sub Do_Dynamic()

         Select Case EngineConfiguration


            Case "cncmdrs"


                  Set cn = CreateObject("ADODB.Connection")
                  Set cmd = CreateObject("ADODB.Command")
                  Set rs = CreateObject("ADODB.Recordset")


                  cn.ConnectionString = "Provider=" & Provider & ";Data Source=" &
fName.Value & ";"
                  Call cn.Open()

                  cmd.ActiveConnection = cn
                  cmd.CommandType = 8
                  cmd.CommandText = strQuery
                  Call cmd.Execute()

                  rs.CursorLocation = 3
                  rs.LockType = 3
                  Call rs.Open(cmd)
```

```
Case "cnrs"

        Set cn = CreateObject("ADODB.Connection")
        Set rs = CreateObject("ADODB.Recordset")

        cn.ConnectionString = "Provider=" & Provider & ";Data Source=" &
fName.Value & ";"
        Call cn.Open()

        rs.ActiveConnection = cn
        rs.CursorLocation = 3
        rs.LockType = 3
        rs.Source = strQuery
        Call rs.Open()

Case "cmdrs"

        Set cmd = CreateObject("ADODB.Command")
        Set rs = CreateObject("ADODB.Recordset")

        cmd.ActiveConnection = "Provider=" & Provider & ";Data Source=" &
fName.Value & ";"
        cmd.CommandType = 8
        cmd.CommandText = strQuery
        Call cmd.Execute()

        rs.CursorLocation = 3
        rs.LockType = 3
        Call rs.Open(cmd)

Case "rs"

      Set rs = CreateObject("ADODB.Recordset")
      rs.ActiveConnection = "Provider=" & Provider & ";Data Source=" &
fName.Value & ";"
      rs.LockType = 3
      rs.Cursorlocation = 3
      rs.Source = strQuery
      Call rs.Open()
```

```vbscript
        End Select

            Set ws = CreateObject("WScript.Shell")
            Set fso = CreateObject("Scripting.FileSystemObject")

            Set txtstream = fso.OpenTextFile(ws.CurrentDirectory & "\" & Tablename &
".html", 2, True, -2)
            txtstream.WriteLine ("<html>")
            txtstream.WriteLine ("<head>")
            txtstream.WriteLine ("<title>" & Tablename & "</title>")

        Add_The_StyleSheet

            txtstream.WriteLine ("</head>")
            txtstream.WriteLine ("<body>")
            txtstream.WriteLine ("<script language='vbscript'>")

            If StyleSheet = "InLine" Then


                Select Case Orientation


                    Case "Single-Line Horizontal"

                        Select Case TableType

                            Case "Table"

                                txtstream.WriteLine    ("document.WriteLn(""<table    Border='1'
cellpadding='1' cellspacing='1' datasrc=#rs>"")")

                            Case "Report"

                                txtstream.WriteLine    ("document.WriteLn(""<table    Border='0'
cellpadding='1' cellspacing='1' datasrc=#rs>"")")

                        End Select
```

```vb
txtstream.WriteLine ("document.WriteLn("""<tr>""")")
For x = 0 To rs.Fields.Count - 1

    txtstream.WriteLine    ("document.WriteLn("""<th    style='font-
family:Calibri, Sans-Serif;font-size: 12px;color:darkred;'>" & rs.Fields(x).Name &
"</th>""")")

Next
txtstream.WriteLine ("document.WriteLn("""</tr>""")")
txtstream.WriteLine ("document.WriteLn("""<tr>""")")
For x = 0 To rs.Fields.Count - 1


    Select Case ControlType

        Case "None"
        txtstream.WriteLine    ("document.WriteLn("""<td    style='font-
family:Calibri, Sans-Serif;font-size: 12px;color:navy;'>" & rs.Fields(x).Value &
"</td>""")")
        Case "Button"
        txtstream.WriteLine    ("document.WriteLn("""<td    style='font-
family:Calibri, Sans-Serif;font-size: 12px;color:navy;'><input type=button Value='"
& rs.Fields(x).Value & "'></input></td>""")")
        Case "Combobox"
        txtstream.WriteLine    ("document.WriteLn("""<td    style='font-
family:Calibri, Sans-Serif;font-size: 12px;color:navy;'><select><option Value='" &
rs.Fields(x).Value & "'>" & rs.Fields(x).Value & "</option></select></td>""")")
        Case "Div"
        txtstream.WriteLine    ("document.WriteLn("""<td    style='font-
family:Calibri, Sans-Serif;font-size: 12px;color:navy;'><div>" & rs.Fields(x).Value &
"</div></td>""")")
        Case "Listbox"
        txtstream.WriteLine    ("document.WriteLn("""<td    style='font-
family:Calibri,        Sans-Serif;font-size:        12px;color:navy;'><select
multiple=true><option Value ='" & rs.Fields(x).Value & "'>" & rs.Fields(x).Value &
"</option></select></td>""")")
        Case "Span"
        txtstream.WriteLine    ("document.WriteLn("""<td    style='font-
family:Calibri, Sans-Serif;font-size: 12px;color:navy;'><span>" & rs.Fields(x).Value
& "</span></td>""")")
```

```
                    Case "Textbox"
            txtstream.WriteLine        ("document.WriteLn(""<td        style='font-
family:Calibri, Sans-Serif;font-size: 12px;color:navy;'><input type=text Value='" &
rs.Fields(x).Value & "'></input></td>"")")
                    Case "Textarea"
            txtstream.WriteLine        ("document.WriteLn(""<td        style='font-
family:Calibri,    Sans-Serif;font-size:    12px;color:navy;'><textarea>"    &
rs.Fields(x).Value & "</textarea></td>"")")

        End Select


    Next

    txtstream.WriteLine ("document.WriteLn(""</tr>"")")


Case "Multi-Line Horizontal"


    Select Case TableType

        Case "Table"

            txtstream.WriteLine    ("document.WriteLn(""<table    Border='1'
cellpadding='1' cellspacing='1'>"")")

        Case "Report"

            txtstream.WriteLine    ("document.WriteLn(""<table    Border='0'
cellpadding='1' cellspacing='1'>"")")

    End Select

    txtstream.WriteLine ("document.WriteLn(""<tr>"")")
    For x = 0 To rs.Fields.Count - 1
```

```
        txtstream.WriteLine    ("document.WriteLn(""<th    style='font-
family:Calibri, Sans-Serif;font-size: 12px;color:darkred;'>" & rs.Fields(x).Name &
"</th>"")")

            Next
            txtstream.WriteLine ("document.WriteLn(""</tr>"")")
            Do While rs.EOF = False

              txtstream.WriteLine ("document.WriteLn(""<tr>"")")
              For x = 0 To rs.Fields.Count - 1

                Select Case ControlType

                  Case "None"
                  txtstream.WriteLine    ("document.WriteLn(""<td    style='font-
family:Calibri, Sans-Serif;font-size: 12px;color:navy;'>" & rs.Fields(x).Value &
"</td>"")")
                  Case "Button"
                  txtstream.WriteLine    ("document.WriteLn(""<td    style='font-
family:Calibri, Sans-Serif;font-size: 12px;color:navy;'><input type=button Value='"
& rs.Fields(x).Value & "'></input></td>"")")
                  Case "Combobox"
                  txtstream.WriteLine    ("document.WriteLn(""<td    style='font-
family:Calibri, Sans-Serif;font-size: 12px;color:navy;'><select><option Value='" &
rs.Fields(x).Value & "'>" & rs.Fields(x).Value & "</option></select></td>"")")
                  Case "Div"
                  txtstream.WriteLine    ("document.WriteLn(""<td    style='font-
family:Calibri, Sans-Serif;font-size: 12px;color:navy;'><div>" & rs.Fields(x).Value &
"</div></td>"")")
                  Case "Listbox"
                  txtstream.WriteLine    ("document.WriteLn(""<td    style='font-
family:Calibri,        Sans-Serif;font-size:        12px;color:navy;'><select
multiple=true><option Value ='" & rs.Fields(x).Value & "'>" & rs.Fields(x).Value &
"</option></select></td>"")")
                  Case "Span"
                  txtstream.WriteLine    ("document.WriteLn(""<td    style='font-
family:Calibri, Sans-Serif;font-size: 12px;color:navy;'><span>" & rs.Fields(x).Value
& "</span></td>"")")
                  Case "Textbox"
```

```vb
            txtstream.WriteLine     ("document.WriteLn(""<td     style='font-
family:Calibri, Sans-Serif;font-size: 12px;color:navy;'><input type=text Value='" &
rs.Fields(x).Value & "'></input></td>"")")
                Case "Textarea"
            txtstream.WriteLine     ("document.WriteLn(""<td     style='font-
family:Calibri,     Sans-Serif;font-size:     12px;color:navy;'><textarea>"     &
rs.Fields(x).Value & "</textarea></td>"")")

            End Select


        Next
        txtstream.WriteLine ("document.WriteLn(""</tr>"")")
        rs.MoveNext
    Loop


    Case "Single-Line Vertical"


    Select Case TableType

        Case "Table"

            txtstream.WriteLine     ("document.WriteLn(""<table   Border='1'
cellpadding='1' cellspacing='1'>"")")

        Case "Report"

            txtstream.WriteLine     ("document.WriteLn(""<table   Border='0'
cellpadding='1' cellspacing='1'>"")")

    End Select

    For x = 0 To rs.Fields.Count - 1

    Select Case ControlType

        Case "None"
```

```vb
        txtstream.WriteLine        ("document.WriteLn(""<tr><th        style='font-
family:Calibri, Sans-Serif;font-size: 12px;color:darkred;'>" & rs.Fields(x).Name &
"</th><td style='font-family:Calibri, Sans-Serif;font-size: 12px;color:navy;'>" &
rs.Fields(x).Value & "</td></tr>""")")
                Case "Button"
        txtstream.WriteLine        ("document.WriteLn(""<tr><th        style='font-
family:Calibri, Sans-Serif;font-size: 12px;color:darkred;'>" & rs.Fields(x).Name &
"</th><td style='font-family:Calibri, Sans-Serif;font-size: 12px;color:navy;'><input
type=button Value='" & rs.Fields(x).Value & "'></input></td></tr>""")")
                Case "Combobox"
        txtstream.WriteLine        ("document.WriteLn(""<tr><th        style='font-
family:Calibri, Sans-Serif;font-size: 12px;color:darkred;'>" & rs.Fields(x).Name &
"</th>          <td          style='font-family:Calibri,          Sans-Serif;font-size:
12px;color:navy;'><select><option    Value='"    &    rs.Fields(x).Value    &    "'>"    &
rs.Fields(x).Value & "</option></select></td></tr>""")")
                Case "Div"
        txtstream.WriteLine        ("document.WriteLn(""<tr><th        style='font-
family:Calibri, Sans-Serif;font-size: 12px;color:darkred;'>" & rs.Fields(x).Name &
"</th><td style='font-family:Calibri, Sans-Serif;font-size: 12px;color:navy;'><div>"
& rs.Fields(x).Value & "</div></td></tr>""")")
                Case "Listbox"
        txtstream.WriteLine        ("document.WriteLn(""<tr><th        style='font-
family:Calibri, Sans-Serif;font-size: 12px;color:darkred;'>" & rs.Fields(x).Name &
"</th><td style='font-family:Calibri, Sans-Serif;font-size: 12px;color:navy;'><select
multiple=true><option Value ='" & rs.Fields(x).Value & "'>" & rs.Fields(x).Value &
"</option></select></td></tr>""")")
                Case "Span"
        txtstream.WriteLine        ("document.WriteLn(""<tr><th        style='font-
family:Calibri, Sans-Serif;font-size: 12px;color:darkred;'>" & rs.Fields(x).Name &
"</th><td          style='font-family:Calibri,          Sans-Serif;font-size:
12px;color:navy;'><span>" & rs.Fields(x).Value & "</span></td></tr>""")")
                Case "Textbox"
        txtstream.WriteLine        ("document.WriteLn(""<tr><th        style='font-
family:Calibri, Sans-Serif;font-size: 12px;color:darkred;'>" & rs.Fields(x).Name &
"</th><td style='font-family:Calibri, Sans-Serif;font-size: 12px;color:navy;'><input
type=text Value='" & rs.Fields(x).Value & "'></input></td></tr>""")")
                Case "Textarea"
        txtstream.WriteLine        ("document.WriteLn(""<tr><th        style='font-
family:Calibri, Sans-Serif;font-size: 12px;color:darkred;'>" & rs.Fields(x).Name &
```

```
"</th><td                style='font-family:Calibri,              Sans-Serif;font-size:
12px;color:navy;'><textarea>" & rs.Fields(x).Value & "</textarea></td></tr>""")")

                    End Select

                Next

            Case "Multi-Line Vertical"

                Select Case TableType

                    Case "Table"

                        txtstream.WriteLine  ("document.WriteLn(""<table  Border='1'
cellpadding='1' cellspacing='1'>""")")

                    Case "Report"

                        txtstream.WriteLine  ("document.WriteLn(""<table  Border='0'
cellpadding='1' cellspacing='1'>""")")

                End Select


                For x = 0 To rs.Fields.Count - 1

                        txtstream.WriteLine  ("document.WriteLn(""<tr><th  style='font-
family:Calibri, Sans-Serif;font-size: 12px;color:darkred;'>" & rs.Fields(x).Name &
"</th>""")")

                    rs.MoveFirst

                    Do While rs.EOF = False


                        Select Case ControlType

                            Case "None"
```

```
                txtstream.WriteLine        ("document.WriteLn(""<td        style='font-
family:Calibri,   Sans-Serif;font-size:   12px;color:navy;'>"   &   rs.Fields(x).Value   &
"</td>"")")
                        Case "Button"
                txtstream.WriteLine        ("document.WriteLn(""<td        style='font-
family:Calibri, Sans-Serif;font-size: 12px;color:navy;'><input type=button Value='"
& rs.Fields(x).Value & "'></input></td>"")")
                        Case "Combobox"
                txtstream.WriteLine        ("document.WriteLn(""<td        style='font-
family:Calibri,   Sans-Serif;font-size:   12px;color:navy;'><select><option Value='"  &
rs.Fields(x).Value & "'>" & rs.Fields(x).Value & "</option></select></td>"")")
                        Case "Div"
                txtstream.WriteLine        ("document.WriteLn(""<td        style='font-
family:Calibri, Sans-Serif;font-size: 12px;color:navy;'><div>" & rs.Fields(x).Value &
"</div></td>"")")
                        Case "Listbox"
                txtstream.WriteLine        ("document.WriteLn(""<td        style='font-
family:Calibri,            Sans-Serif;font-size:            12px;color:navy;'><select
multiple=true><option Value ='" & rs.Fields(x).Value & "'>" & rs.Fields(x).Value &
"</option></select></td>"")")
                        Case "Span"
                txtstream.WriteLine        ("document.WriteLn(""<td        style='font-
family:Calibri, Sans-Serif;font-size: 12px;color:navy;'><span>" & rs.Fields(x).Value
& "</span></td>"")")
                        Case "Textbox"
                txtstream.WriteLine        ("document.WriteLn(""<td        style='font-
family:Calibri, Sans-Serif;font-size: 12px;color:navy;'><input type=text Value='" &
rs.Fields(x).Value & "'></input></td>"")")
                        Case "Textarea"
                txtstream.WriteLine        ("document.WriteLn(""<td        style='font-
family:Calibri,       Sans-Serif;font-size:       12px;color:navy;'><textarea>"       &
rs.Fields(x).Value & "</textarea></td>"")")


                End Select

                rs.MoveNext

            Loop

            txtstream.WriteLine ("document.WriteLn(""</tr>"")")
```

```
                    Next


            End Select


        Else


            Select Case Orientation


                Case "Single-Line Horizontal"

                Select Case TableType

                    Case "Table"

                        txtstream.WriteLine   ("document.WriteLn(""<table  Border='1'
cellpadding='1' cellspacing='1' datasrc=#rs>"")")

                    Case "Report"

                        txtstream.WriteLine   ("document.WriteLn(""<table  Border='0'
cellpadding='1' cellspacing='1' datasrc=#rs>"")")

                End Select


                txtstream.WriteLine ("document.WriteLn(""<tr>"")")
                For x = 0 To rs.Fields.Count - 1

                    txtstream.WriteLine        ("document.WriteLn(""<th>"          &
rs.Fields(x).Name & "</th>"")")

                Next
                txtstream.WriteLine ("document.WriteLn(""</tr>"")")
                txtstream.WriteLine ("document.WriteLn(""<tr>"")")
```

```vb
For x = 0 To rs.Fields.Count - 1

    Select Case ControlType

        Case "None"
    txtstream.WriteLine ("document.WriteLn(""<td>" & rs.Fields(x).Value
& "</td>"")")
        Case "Button"
    txtstream.WriteLine  ("document.WriteLn(""<td><input   type=button
Value='" & rs.Fields(x).Value & "'></input></td>"")")
        Case "Combobox"
    txtstream.WriteLine        ("document.WriteLn(""<td><select><option
Value='"     &     rs.Fields(x).Value    &    "'>"    &    rs.Fields(x).Value    &
"</option></select></td>"")")
        Case "Div"
    txtstream.WriteLine         ("document.WriteLn(""<td><div>"        &
rs.Fields(x).Value & "</div></td>"")")
        Case "Listbox"
    txtstream.WriteLine                 ("document.WriteLn(""<td><select
multiple=true><option Value ='" & rs.Fields(x).Value & "'>" & rs.Fields(x).Value &
"</option></select></td>"")")
        Case "Span"
    txtstream.WriteLine        ("document.WriteLn(""<td><span>"        &
rs.Fields(x).Value & "</span></td>"")")
        Case "Textbox"
    txtstream.WriteLine   ("document.WriteLn(""<td><input    type=text
Value='" & rs.Fields(x).Value & "'></input></td>"")")
        Case "Textarea"
    txtstream.WriteLine       ("document.WriteLn(""<td><textarea>"      &
rs.Fields(x).Value & "</textarea></td>"")")

    End Select


Next

    txtstream.WriteLine ("document.WriteLn(""</tr>"")")
```

```vb
Case "Multi-Line Horizontal"

        Select Case TableType

            Case "Table"

                txtstream.WriteLine    ("document.WriteLn(""<table  Border='1'
cellpadding='1' cellspacing='1'>"")")

                Case "Report"

                txtstream.WriteLine    ("document.WriteLn(""<table  Border='0'
cellpadding='1' cellspacing='1'>"")")

        End Select

        txtstream.WriteLine ("document.WriteLn(""<tr>"")")
        For x = 0 To rs.Fields.Count - 1

                txtstream.WriteLine           ("document.WriteLn(""<th>"        &
rs.Fields(x).Name & "</th>"")")

        Next
        txtstream.WriteLine ("document.WriteLn(""</tr>"")")
        Do While rs.EOF = False

            txtstream.WriteLine ("document.WriteLn(""<tr>"")")
            For x = 0 To rs.Fields.Count - 1

                Select Case ControlType

                    Case "None"
                    txtstream.WriteLine           ("document.WriteLn(""<td>"      &
rs.Fields(x).Value & "</td>"")")
                    Case "Button"
                    txtstream.WriteLine ("document.WriteLn(""<td><input type=button
Value='" & rs.Fields(x).Value & "'></input></td>"")")
                    Case "Combobox"
```

```
                txtstream.WriteLine        ("document.WriteLn(""<td><select><option
Value='"    &    rs.Fields(x).Value    &    "'>"   &   rs.Fields(x).Value    &
"</option></select></td>"")")
                    Case "Div"
                txtstream.WriteLine        ("document.WriteLn(""<td><div>"       &
rs.Fields(x).Value & "</div></td>"")")
                    Case "Listbox"
                txtstream.WriteLine            ("document.WriteLn(""<td><select
multiple=true><option Value ='" & rs.Fields(x).Value & "'>" & rs.Fields(x).Value &
"</option></select></td>"")")
                    Case "Span"
                txtstream.WriteLine        ("document.WriteLn(""<td><span>"       &
rs.Fields(x).Value & "</span></td>"")")
                    Case "Textbox"
                txtstream.WriteLine   ("document.WriteLn(""<td><input    type=text
Value='" & rs.Fields(x).Value & "'></input></td>"")")
                    Case "Textarea"
                txtstream.WriteLine        ("document.WriteLn(""<td><textarea>"     &
rs.Fields(x).Value & "</textarea></td>"")")

                End Select


            Next
            txtstream.WriteLine ("document.WriteLn(""</tr>"")")
            rs.MoveNext
        Loop



        Case "Single-Line Vertical"


        Select Case TableType


        Case "Table"

            txtstream.WriteLine   ("document.WriteLn(""<table   Border='1'
cellpadding='1' cellspacing='1'>"")")
```

```vb
Case "Report"

        txtstream.WriteLine ("document.WriteLn(""<table Border='0'
cellpadding='1' cellspacing='1'>"")")

    End Select

    For x = 0 To rs.Fields.Count - 1

        Select Case ControlType

            Case "None"
                txtstream.WriteLine        ("document.WriteLn(""<tr><th>"        &
rs.Fields(x).Name & "</th><td>" & rs.Fields(x).Value & "</td></tr>"")")
            Case "Button"
                txtstream.WriteLine        ("document.WriteLn(""<tr><th>"        &
rs.Fields(x).Name & "</th><td><input type=button Value='" & rs.Fields(x).Value &
"'></input></td></tr>"")")
            Case "Combobox"
                txtstream.WriteLine        ("document.WriteLn(""<tr><th>"        &
rs.Fields(x).Name & "</th> <td><select><option Value='" & rs.Fields(x).Value &
"'>" & rs.Fields(x).Value & "</option></select></td></tr>"")")
            Case "Div"
                txtstream.WriteLine        ("document.WriteLn(""<tr><th>"        &
rs.Fields(x).Name      &      "</th><td><div>"      &      rs.Fields(x).Value      &
"</div></td></tr>"")")
            Case "Listbox"
                txtstream.WriteLine        ("document.WriteLn(""<tr><th>"        &
rs.Fields(x).Name   &   "</th><td><select   multiple=true><option   Value   ='"   &
rs.Fields(x).Value & "'>" & rs.Fields(x).Value & "</option></select></td></tr>"")")
            Case "Span"
                txtstream.WriteLine        ("document.WriteLn(""<tr><th>"        &
rs.Fields(x).Name      &      "</th><td><span>"      &      rs.Fields(x).Value      &
"</span></td></tr>"")")
            Case "Textbox"
                txtstream.WriteLine        ("document.WriteLn(""<tr><th>"        &
rs.Fields(x).Name & "</th><td><input type=text Value='" & rs.Fields(x).Value &
"'></input></td></tr>"")")
            Case "Textarea"
```

```
            txtstream.WriteLine        ("document.WriteLn(""<tr><th>"        &
rs.Fields(x).Name       &       "</th><td><textarea>"       &       rs.Fields(x).Value       &
"</textarea></td></tr>"")")

                End Select

            Next


        Case "Multi-Line Vertical"


            Select Case TableType

                Case "Table"

                    txtstream.WriteLine ("document.WriteLn(""<table   Border='1'
cellpadding='1' cellspacing='1'>"")")

                Case "Report"

                    txtstream.WriteLine ("document.WriteLn(""<table   Border='0'
cellpadding='1' cellspacing='1'>"")")

            End Select


            For x = 0 To rs.Fields.Count - 1

                txtstream.WriteLine        ("document.WriteLn(""<tr><th>"        &
rs.Fields(x).Name & "</th>"")")

                rs.MoveFirst

                Do While rs.EOF = False


                    Select Case ControlType

                        Case "None"
```

```
                    txtstream.WriteLine          ("document.WriteLn(""<td>"          &
rs.Fields(x).Value & "</td>"")")
                    Case "Button"
                    txtstream.WriteLine ("document.WriteLn(""<td><input type=button
Value='" & rs.Fields(x).Value & "'></input></td>"")")
                    Case "Combobox"
                    txtstream.WriteLine     ("document.WriteLn(""<td><select><option
Value='"     &    rs.Fields(x).Value    &    "'>"    &    rs.Fields(x).Value    &
"</option></select></td>"")")
                    Case "Div"
                    txtstream.WriteLine          ("document.WriteLn(""<td><div>"          &
rs.Fields(x).Value & "</div></td>"")")
                    Case "Listbox"
                    txtstream.WriteLine                ("document.WriteLn(""<td><select
multiple=true><option Value ='" & rs.Fields(x).Value & "'>" & rs.Fields(x).Value &
"</option></select></td>"")")
                    Case "Span"
                    txtstream.WriteLine     ("document.WriteLn(""<td><span>"          &
rs.Fields(x).Value & "</span></td>"")")
                    Case "Textbox"
                    txtstream.WriteLine ("document.WriteLn(""<td><input   type=text
Value='" & rs.Fields(x).Value & "'></input></td>"")")
                    Case "Textarea"
                    txtstream.WriteLine     ("document.WriteLn(""<td><textarea>"          &
rs.Fields(x).Value & "</textarea></td>"")")

                    End Select

                    rs.MoveNext

              Loop

              txtstream.WriteLine ("document.WriteLn(""</tr>"")")

        Next


        End Select
```

```
        End If

        txtstream.WriteLine ("document.WriteLn(""</table>"")")
        txtstream.WriteLine (Chr(60) & "/script>")
        txtstream.WriteLine ("</body>")
        txtstream.WriteLine ("</html>")
        txtstream.Close


        tempstr = ""
        Set txtstream = fso.OpenTextFile(ws.CurrentDirectory & "\" & Tablename &
".html", 1, True, -2)
        Do While txtstream.AtEndOfStream = False
           tempstr = tempstr & txtstream.ReadLine()
           tempstr = tempstr & vbCrLf
        Loop
        txtstream.Close
        textarea1.innerText = tempstr

    End Sub

    Sub Do_Cloaked()


      Select Case EngineConfiguration


         Case "cncmdrs"


              Set cn = CreateObject("ADODB.Connection")
              Set cmd = CreateObject("ADODB.Command")
              Set rs = CreateObject("ADODB.Recordset")


              cn.ConnectionString = "Provider=" & Provider & ";Data Source=" &
fName.Value & ";"
              Call cn.Open()

              cmd.ActiveConnection = cn
```

```
                cmd.CommandType = 8
                cmd.CommandText = strQuery
                Call cmd.Execute()

                rs.CursorLocation = 3
                rs.LockType = 3
                Call rs.Open(cmd)


        Case "cnrs"

                Set cn = CreateObject("ADODB.Connection")
                Set rs = CreateObject("ADODB.Recordset")

                cn.ConnectionString = "Provider=" & Provider & ";Data Source=" &
        fName.Value & ";"
                Call cn.Open()

                rs.ActiveConnection = cn
                rs.CursorLocation = 3
                rs.LockType = 3
                rs.Source = strQuery
                Call rs.Open()

        Case "cmdrs"

                Set cmd = CreateObject("ADODB.Command")
                Set rs = CreateObject("ADODB.Recordset")

                cmd.ActiveConnection = "Provider=" & Provider & ";Data Source=" &
        fName.Value & ";"
                cmd.CommandType = 8
                cmd.CommandText = strQuery
                Call cmd.Execute()

                rs.CursorLocation = 3
                rs.LockType = 3
                Call rs.Open(cmd)

        Case "rs"
```

```
            Set rs = CreateObject("ADODB.Recordset")
            rs.ActiveConnection = "Provider=" & Provider & ";Data Source=" &
fName.Value & ";"
            rs.LockType = 3
            rs.Cursorlocation = 3
            rs.Source = strQuery
            Call rs.Open()

      End Select


         Set ws = CreateObject("WScript.Shell")
         Set fso = CreateObject("Scripting.FileSystemObject")

         Set txtstream = fso.OpenTextFile(ws.CurrentDirectory & "\" & Tablename &
".html", 2, True, -2)
         txtstream.WriteLine ("<html>")
         txtstream.WriteLine ("<head>")
         txtstream.WriteLine ("<title>" & Tablename & "</title>")

      Add_The_StyleSheet

         txtstream.WriteLine ("</head>")
         txtstream.WriteLine ("<body>")
         txtstream.WriteLine ("<script language='vbscript'>")
         txtstream.WriteLine ("")
         txtstream.WriteLine ("dim mystr")
         txtstream.WriteLine ("")
         txtstream.WriteLine ("Sub Window_OnLoad()")
         txtstream.WriteLine ("")

         If StyleSheet = "InLine" Then


            Select Case Orientation


                Case "Single-Line Horizontal"
```

```vb
Select Case TableType

        Case "Table"

                txtstream.WriteLine ("mystr = mystr & ""<table Border='1'
cellpadding='1' cellspacing='1' datasrc=#rs>"" & vbcrlf")

        Case "Report"

                txtstream.WriteLine ("mystr = mystr & ""<table Border='0'
cellpadding='1' cellspacing='1' datasrc=#rs>"" & vbcrlf")

        End Select

        txtstream.WriteLine ("mystr = mystr & ""<tr>"" & vbcrlf")
        For x = 0 To rs.Fields.Count - 1

                txtstream.WriteLine ("mystr = mystr & ""<th style='font-
family:Calibri, Sans-Serif;font-size: 12px;color:darkred;'>" & rs.Fields(x).Name &
"</th>"" & vbcrlf")

        Next
        txtstream.WriteLine ("mystr = mystr & ""</tr>"" & vbcrlf")
        txtstream.WriteLine ("mystr = mystr & ""<tr>"" & vbcrlf")
        For x = 0 To rs.Fields.Count - 1


        Select Case ControlType

                Case "None"
        txtstream.WriteLine ("mystr = mystr & ""<td style='font-
family:Calibri, Sans-Serif;font-size: 12px;color:navy;'>" & rs.Fields(x).Value &
"</td>"" & vbcrlf")
                Case "Button"
        txtstream.WriteLine ("mystr = mystr & ""<td style='font-
family:Calibri, Sans-Serif;font-size: 12px;color:navy;'><input type=button Value='"
& rs.Fields(x).Value & "'></input></td>"" & vbcrlf")
                Case "Combobox"
```

```
            txtstream.WriteLine ("mystr = mystr & ""<td style='font-
family:Calibri, Sans-Serif;font-size: 12px;color:navy;'><select><option Value='" &
rs.Fields(x).Value & "'>" & rs.Fields(x).Value & "</option></select></td>"" &
vbcrlf")
                Case "Div"
            txtstream.WriteLine ("mystr = mystr & ""<td style='font-
family:Calibri, Sans-Serif;font-size: 12px;color:navy;'><div>" & rs.Fields(x).Value &
"</div></td>"" & vbcrlf")
                Case "Listbox"
            txtstream.WriteLine ("mystr = mystr & ""<td style='font-
family:Calibri,          Sans-Serif;font-size:          12px;color:navy;'><select
multiple=true><option Value ='" & rs.Fields(x).Value & "'>" & rs.Fields(x).Value &
"</option></select></td>"" & vbcrlf")
                Case "Span"
            txtstream.WriteLine ("mystr = mystr & ""<td style='font-
family:Calibri, Sans-Serif;font-size: 12px;color:navy;'><span>" & rs.Fields(x).Value
& "</span></td>"" & vbcrlf")
                Case "Textbox"
            txtstream.WriteLine ("mystr = mystr & ""<td style='font-
family:Calibri, Sans-Serif;font-size: 12px;color:navy;'><input type=text Value='" &
rs.Fields(x).Value & "'></input></td>"" & vbcrlf")
                Case "Textarea"
            txtstream.WriteLine ("mystr = mystr & ""<td style='font-
family:Calibri,     Sans-Serif;font-size:     12px;color:navy;'><textarea>"     &
rs.Fields(x).Value & "</textarea></td>"" & vbcrlf")

            End Select


            Next

            txtstream.WriteLine ("mystr = mystr & ""</tr>"" & vbcrlf")


        Case "Multi-Line Horizontal"


            Select Case TableType
```

```vb
        Case "Table"

            txtstream.WriteLine ("mystr = mystr & ""<table Border='1'
cellpadding='1' cellspacing='1'>"" & vbcrlf")

        Case "Report"

            txtstream.WriteLine ("mystr = mystr & ""<table Border='0'
cellpadding='1' cellspacing='1'>"" & vbcrlf")

    End Select

    txtstream.WriteLine ("mystr = mystr & ""<tr>"" & vbcrlf")
    For x = 0 To rs.Fields.Count - 1

        txtstream.WriteLine ("mystr = mystr & ""<th style='font-
family:Calibri, Sans-Serif;font-size: 12px;color:darkred;'>" & rs.Fields(x).Name &
"</th>"" & vbcrlf")

    Next
    txtstream.WriteLine ("mystr = mystr & ""</tr>"" & vbcrlf")
    Do While rs.EOF = False

        txtstream.WriteLine ("mystr = mystr & ""<tr>"" & vbcrlf")
        For x = 0 To rs.Fields.Count - 1

        Select Case ControlType

            Case "None"
            txtstream.WriteLine ("mystr = mystr & ""<td style='font-
family:Calibri, Sans-Serif;font-size: 12px;color:navy;'>" & rs.Fields(x).Value &
"</td>"" & vbcrlf")
            Case "Button"
            txtstream.WriteLine ("mystr = mystr & ""<td style='font-
family:Calibri, Sans-Serif;font-size: 12px;color:navy;'><input type=button Value='"
& rs.Fields(x).Value & "'></input></td>"" & vbcrlf")
            Case "Combobox"
            txtstream.WriteLine ("mystr = mystr & ""<td style='font-
family:Calibri, Sans-Serif;font-size: 12px;color:navy;'><select><option Value='" &
```

rs.Fields(x).Value & "'>" & rs.Fields(x).Value & "</option></select></td>"" & vbcrlf")

                Case "Div"

            txtstream.WriteLine ("mystr = mystr & ""<td style='font-family:Calibri, Sans-Serif;font-size: 12px;color:navy;'> " & rs.Fields(x).Value & " </td>"" & vbcrlf")

                Case "Listbox"

            txtstream.WriteLine ("mystr = mystr & ""<td style='font-family:Calibri, Sans-Serif;font-size: 12px;color:navy;'><select multiple=true><option Value ='" & rs.Fields(x).Value & "'>" & rs.Fields(x).Value & "</option></select></td>"" & vbcrlf")

                Case "Span"

            txtstream.WriteLine ("mystr = mystr & ""<td style='font-family:Calibri, Sans-Serif;font-size: 12px;color:navy;'>" & rs.Fields(x).Value & "</td>"" & vbcrlf")

                Case "Textbox"

            txtstream.WriteLine ("mystr = mystr & ""<td style='font-family:Calibri, Sans-Serif;font-size: 12px;color:navy;'><input type=text Value='" & rs.Fields(x).Value & "'></input></td>"" & vbcrlf")

                Case "Textarea"

            txtstream.WriteLine ("mystr = mystr & ""<td style='font-family:Calibri, Sans-Serif;font-size: 12px;color:navy;'><textarea>" & rs.Fields(x).Value & "</textarea></td>"" & vbcrlf")

            End Select

        Next
        txtstream.WriteLine ("mystr = mystr & ""</tr>"" & vbcrlf")
        rs.MoveNext
      Loop

      Case "Single-Line Vertical"

      Select Case TableType

        Case "Table"

```vb
            txtstream.WriteLine ("mystr = mystr & ""<table Border='1'
cellpadding='1' cellspacing='1'>"" & vbcrlf")

        Case "Report"

            txtstream.WriteLine ("mystr = mystr & ""<table Border='0'
cellpadding='1' cellspacing='1'>"" & vbcrlf")

        End Select

        For x = 0 To rs.Fields.Count - 1

        Select Case ControlType

            Case "None"
            txtstream.WriteLine ("mystr = mystr & ""<tr><th style='font-
family:Calibri, Sans-Serif;font-size: 12px;color:darkred;'>" & rs.Fields(x).Name &
"</th><td style='font-family:Calibri, Sans-Serif;font-size: 12px;color:navy;'>" &
rs.Fields(x).Value & "</td></tr>"" & vbcrlf")
            Case "Button"
            txtstream.WriteLine ("mystr = mystr & ""<tr><th style='font-
family:Calibri, Sans-Serif;font-size: 12px;color:darkred;'>" & rs.Fields(x).Name &
"</th><td style='font-family:Calibri, Sans-Serif;font-size: 12px;color:navy;'><input
type=button Value='" & rs.Fields(x).Value & "'></input></td></tr>"" & vbcrlf")
            Case "Combobox"
            txtstream.WriteLine ("mystr = mystr & ""<tr><th style='font-
family:Calibri, Sans-Serif;font-size: 12px;color:darkred;'>" & rs.Fields(x).Name &
"</th>        <td        style='font-family:Calibri,        Sans-Serif;font-size:
12px;color:navy;'><select><option Value='" & rs.Fields(x).Value & "'>" &
rs.Fields(x).Value & "</option></select></td></tr>"" & vbcrlf")
            Case "Div"
            txtstream.WriteLine ("mystr = mystr & ""<tr><th style='font-
family:Calibri, Sans-Serif;font-size: 12px;color:darkred;'>" & rs.Fields(x).Name &
"</th><td style='font-family:Calibri, Sans-Serif;font-size: 12px;color:navy;'><div>"
& rs.Fields(x).Value & "</div></td></tr>"" & vbcrlf")
            Case "Listbox"
            txtstream.WriteLine ("mystr = mystr & ""<tr><th style='font-
family:Calibri, Sans-Serif;font-size: 12px;color:darkred;'>" & rs.Fields(x).Name &
"</th><td style='font-family:Calibri, Sans-Serif;font-size: 12px;color:navy;'><select
```

```vb
multiple=true><option Value ='" & rs.Fields(x).Value & "'>" & rs.Fields(x).Value &
"</option></select></td></tr>"" & vbcrlf")
                    Case "Span"
                txtstream.WriteLine ("mystr = mystr & ""<tr><th style='font-
family:Calibri, Sans-Serif;font-size: 12px;color:darkred;'>" & rs.Fields(x).Name &
"</th><td            style='font-family:Calibri,            Sans-Serif;font-size:
12px;color:navy;'><span>" & rs.Fields(x).Value & "</span></td></tr>"" & vbcrlf")
                    Case "Textbox"
                txtstream.WriteLine ("mystr = mystr & ""<tr><th style='font-
family:Calibri, Sans-Serif;font-size: 12px;color:darkred;'>" & rs.Fields(x).Name &
"</th><td style='font-family:Calibri, Sans-Serif;font-size: 12px;color:navy;'><input
type=text Value='" & rs.Fields(x).Value & "'></input></td></tr>"" & vbcrlf")
                    Case "Textarea"
                txtstream.WriteLine ("mystr = mystr & ""<tr><th style='font-
family:Calibri, Sans-Serif;font-size: 12px;color:darkred;'>" & rs.Fields(x).Name &
"</th><td            style='font-family:Calibri,            Sans-Serif;font-size:
12px;color:navy;'><textarea>" & rs.Fields(x).Value & "</textarea></td></tr>"" &
vbcrlf")

            End Select

        Next


        Case "Multi-Line Vertical"


            Select Case TableType

            Case "Table"

                txtstream.WriteLine ("mystr = mystr & ""<table Border='1'
cellpadding='1' cellspacing='1'>"" & vbcrlf")

            Case "Report"

                txtstream.WriteLine ("mystr = mystr & ""<table Border='0'
cellpadding='1' cellspacing='1'>"" & vbcrlf")

            End Select
```

For x = 0 To rs.Fields.Count - 1

txtstream.WriteLine ("mystr = mystr & ""<tr><th style='font-family:Calibri, Sans-Serif;font-size: 12px;color:darkred;'>" & rs.Fields(x).Name & "</th>""" & vbcrlf")

rs.MoveFirst

Do While rs.EOF = False

Select Case ControlType

Case "None"
txtstream.WriteLine ("mystr = mystr & ""<td style='font-family:Calibri, Sans-Serif;font-size: 12px;color:navy;'>" & rs.Fields(x).Value & "</td>""" & vbcrlf")
Case "Button"
txtstream.WriteLine ("mystr = mystr & ""<td style='font-family:Calibri, Sans-Serif;font-size: 12px;color:navy;'><input type=button Value='" & rs.Fields(x).Value & "'></input></td>""" & vbcrlf")
Case "Combobox"
txtstream.WriteLine ("mystr = mystr & ""<td style='font-family:Calibri, Sans-Serif;font-size: 12px;color:navy;'><select><option Value='" & rs.Fields(x).Value & "'>" & rs.Fields(x).Value & "</option></select></td>""" & vbcrlf")
Case "Div"
txtstream.WriteLine ("mystr = mystr & ""<td style='font-family:Calibri, Sans-Serif;font-size: 12px;color:navy;'> " & rs.Fields(x).Value & " </td>""" & vbcrlf")
Case "Listbox"
txtstream.WriteLine ("mystr = mystr & ""<td style='font-family:Calibri, Sans-Serif;font-size: 12px;color:navy;'><select multiple=true><option Value ='" & rs.Fields(x).Value & "'>" & rs.Fields(x).Value & "</option></select></td>""" & vbcrlf")
Case "Span"

```
                    txtstream.WriteLine ("mystr = mystr & ""<td style='font-
family:Calibri, Sans-Serif;font-size: 12px;color:navy;'><span>" & rs.Fields(x).Value
& "</span></td>""" & vbcrlf")
                    Case "Textbox"
                    txtstream.WriteLine ("mystr = mystr & ""<td style='font-
family:Calibri, Sans-Serif;font-size: 12px;color:navy;'><input type=text Value='" &
rs.Fields(x).Value & "'></input></td>""" & vbcrlf")
                    Case "Textarea"
                    txtstream.WriteLine ("mystr = mystr & ""<td style='font-
family:Calibri,      Sans-Serif;font-size:      12px;color:navy;'><textarea>"      &
rs.Fields(x).Value & "</textarea></td>""" & vbcrlf")

                End Select

                rs.MoveNext

            Loop

            txtstream.WriteLine ("mystr = mystr & ""</tr>""" & vbcrlf")

        Next


        End Select



    Else


    Select Case Orientation


        Case "Single-Line Horizontal"

        Select Case TableType

            Case "Table"
```

```
                    txtstream.WriteLine ("mystr = mystr & ""<table Border='1'
cellpadding='1' cellspacing='1' datasrc=#rs>"" & vbcrlf")

            Case "Report"

                    txtstream.WriteLine ("mystr = mystr & ""<table Border='0'
cellpadding='1' cellspacing='1' datasrc=#rs>"" & vbcrlf")

        End Select


        txtstream.WriteLine ("mystr = mystr & ""<tr>"" & vbcrlf")
        For x = 0 To rs.Fields.Count - 1

            txtstream.WriteLine    ("mystr    =    mystr    &    ""<th>"    &
rs.Fields(x).Name & "</th>"" & vbcrlf")

        Next
        txtstream.WriteLine ("mystr = mystr & ""</tr>"" & vbcrlf")
        txtstream.WriteLine ("mystr = mystr & ""<tr>"" & vbcrlf")
        For x = 0 To rs.Fields.Count - 1


        Select Case ControlType

            Case "None"
        txtstream.WriteLine ("mystr = mystr & ""<td>" & rs.Fields(x).Value &
"</td>"" & vbcrlf")
            Case "Button"
        txtstream.WriteLine ("mystr = mystr & ""<td><input type=button
Value='" & rs.Fields(x).Value & "'></input></td>"" & vbcrlf")
            Case "Combobox"
        txtstream.WriteLine ("mystr = mystr & ""<td><select><option
Value='"    &    rs.Fields(x).Value    &    "'>"    &    rs.Fields(x).Value    &
"</option></select></td>"" & vbcrlf")
            Case "Div"
        txtstream.WriteLine ("mystr = mystr & ""<td><div>"    &
rs.Fields(x).Value & "</div></td>"" & vbcrlf")
            Case "Listbox"
```

```
            txtstream.WriteLine    ("mystr  =  mystr  &  ""<td><select
multiple=true><option Value ='" & rs.Fields(x).Value & "'>" & rs.Fields(x).Value &
"</option></select></td>"" & vbcrlf")
            Case "Span"
            txtstream.WriteLine   ("mystr  =  mystr  &  ""<td><span>"  &
rs.Fields(x).Value & "</span></td>"" & vbcrlf")
            Case "Textbox"
            txtstream.WriteLine ("mystr = mystr & ""<td><input type=text
Value='" & rs.Fields(x).Value & "'></input></td>"" & vbcrlf")
            Case "Textarea"
            txtstream.WriteLine  ("mystr  =  mystr  &  ""<td><textarea>"  &
rs.Fields(x).Value & "</textarea></td>"" & vbcrlf")

        End Select


    Next

    txtstream.WriteLine ("mystr = mystr & ""</tr>"" & vbcrlf")


    Case "Multi-Line Horizontal"


    Select Case TableType

        Case "Table"

            txtstream.WriteLine ("mystr = mystr & ""<table Border='1'
cellpadding='1' cellspacing='1'>"" & vbcrlf")

        Case "Report"

            txtstream.WriteLine ("mystr = mystr & ""<table Border='0'
cellpadding='1' cellspacing='1'>"" & vbcrlf")

    End Select

    txtstream.WriteLine ("mystr = mystr & ""<tr>"" & vbcrlf")
```

```
For x = 0 To rs.Fields.Count - 1

        txtstream.WriteLine ("mystr  =  mystr  &  ""<th>"  &
rs.Fields(x).Name & "</th>""" & vbcrlf")

    Next
    txtstream.WriteLine ("mystr = mystr & ""</tr>""" & vbcrlf")
    Do While rs.EOF = False

        txtstream.WriteLine ("mystr = mystr & ""<tr>""" & vbcrlf")
        For x = 0 To rs.Fields.Count - 1

        Select Case ControlType

            Case "None"
            txtstream.WriteLine ("mystr = mystr & ""<td>" & rs.Fields(x).Value
& "</td>""" & vbcrlf")
                Case "Button"
            txtstream.WriteLine ("mystr = mystr & ""<td><input type=button
Value='" & rs.Fields(x).Value & "'></input></td>""" & vbcrlf")
                Case "Combobox"
            txtstream.WriteLine ("mystr = mystr & ""<td><select><option
Value='"   &   rs.Fields(x).Value   &   "'>"   &   rs.Fields(x).Value   &
"</option></select></td>""" & vbcrlf")
                Case "Div"
            txtstream.WriteLine ("mystr  =  mystr  &  ""<td><div>"  &
rs.Fields(x).Value & "</div></td>""" & vbcrlf")
                Case "Listbox"
            txtstream.WriteLine  ("mystr  =  mystr  &  ""<td><select
multiple=true><option Value ='" & rs.Fields(x).Value & "'>" & rs.Fields(x).Value &
"</option></select></td>""" & vbcrlf")
                Case "Span"
            txtstream.WriteLine  ("mystr  =  mystr  &  ""<td><span>"  &
rs.Fields(x).Value & "</span></td>""" & vbcrlf")
                Case "Textbox"
            txtstream.WriteLine ("mystr = mystr & ""<td><input type=text
Value='" & rs.Fields(x).Value & "'></input></td>""" & vbcrlf")
                Case "Textarea"
            txtstream.WriteLine ("mystr = mystr & ""<td><textarea>" &
rs.Fields(x).Value & "</textarea></td>""" & vbcrlf")
```

```
                End Select


            Next
            txtstream.WriteLine ("mystr = mystr & ""</tr>""" & vbcrlf")
            rs.MoveNext
        Loop



    Case "Single-Line Vertical"


        Select Case TableType

            Case "Table"

                txtstream.WriteLine ("mystr = mystr & ""<table Border='1'
cellpadding='1' cellspacing='1'>""" & vbcrlf")

            Case "Report"

                txtstream.WriteLine ("mystr = mystr & ""<table Border='0'
cellpadding='1' cellspacing='1'>""" & vbcrlf")

        End Select

        For x = 0 To rs.Fields.Count - 1

            Select Case ControlType

                Case "None"
            txtstream.WriteLine    ("mystr   =   mystr   &   ""<tr><th>"   &
rs.Fields(x).Name & "</th><td>" & rs.Fields(x).Value & "</td></tr>""" & vbcrlf")
                Case "Button"
            txtstream.WriteLine    ("mystr   =   mystr   &   ""<tr><th>"   &
rs.Fields(x).Name & "</th><td><input type=button Value='" & rs.Fields(x).Value &
"'></input></td></tr>""" & vbcrlf")
                Case "Combobox"
```

```
                txtstream.WriteLine    ("mystr  =  mystr  &  """<tr><th>"  &
rs.Fields(x).Name & "</th> <td><select><option Value='" & rs.Fields(x).Value &
"'>" & rs.Fields(x).Value & "</option></select></td></tr>""" & vbcrlf")
                Case "Div"
                txtstream.WriteLine    ("mystr  =  mystr  &  """<tr><th>"  &
rs.Fields(x).Name & "</th><td><div>" & rs.Fields(x).Value & "</div></td></tr>""" &
vbcrlf")
                Case "Listbox"
                txtstream.WriteLine    ("mystr  =  mystr  &  """<tr><th>"  &
rs.Fields(x).Name  &  "</th><td><select  multiple=true><option  Value  ='"  &
rs.Fields(x).Value & "'>" & rs.Fields(x).Value & "</option></select></td></tr>""" &
vbcrlf")
                Case "Span"
                txtstream.WriteLine    ("mystr  =  mystr  &  """<tr><th>"  &
rs.Fields(x).Name    &    "</th><td><span>"    &    rs.Fields(x).Value    &
"</span></td></tr>""" & vbcrlf")
                Case "Textbox"
                txtstream.WriteLine    ("mystr  =  mystr  &  """<tr><th>"  &
rs.Fields(x).Name & "</th><td><input type=text Value='" & rs.Fields(x).Value &
"'></input></td></tr>""" & vbcrlf")
                Case "Textarea"
                txtstream.WriteLine    ("mystr  =  mystr  &  """<tr><th>"  &
rs.Fields(x).Name    &    "</th><td><textarea>"    &    rs.Fields(x).Value    &
"</textarea></td></tr>""" & vbcrlf")

            End Select

        Next


    Case "Multi-Line Vertical"


        Select Case TableType

        Case "Table"

            txtstream.WriteLine ("mystr = mystr & """<table Border='1'
cellpadding='1' cellspacing='1'>""" & vbcrlf")
```

Case "Report"

txtstream.WriteLine ("mystr = mystr & ""<table Border='0' cellpadding='1' cellspacing='1'>"" & vbcrlf")

End Select

For x = 0 To rs.Fields.Count - 1

txtstream.WriteLine ("mystr = mystr & ""<tr><th>" & rs.Fields(x).Name & "</th>"" & vbcrlf")

rs.MoveFirst

Do While rs.EOF = False

Select Case ControlType

Case "None"
txtstream.WriteLine ("mystr = mystr & ""<td>" & rs.Fields(x).Value & "</td>"" & vbcrlf")
Case "Button"
txtstream.WriteLine ("mystr = mystr & ""<td><input type=button Value='" & rs.Fields(x).Value & "'></input></td>"" & vbcrlf")
Case "Combobox"
txtstream.WriteLine ("mystr = mystr & ""<td><select><option Value='" & rs.Fields(x).Value & "'>" & rs.Fields(x).Value & "</option></select></td>"" & vbcrlf")
Case "Div"
txtstream.WriteLine ("mystr = mystr & ""<td> " & rs.Fields(x).Value & " </td>"" & vbcrlf")
Case "Listbox"
txtstream.WriteLine ("mystr = mystr & ""<td><select multiple=true><option Value ='" & rs.Fields(x).Value & "'>" & rs.Fields(x).Value & "</option></select></td>"" & vbcrlf")
Case "Span"
txtstream.WriteLine ("mystr = mystr & ""<td>" & rs.Fields(x).Value & "</td>"" & vbcrlf")

```vb
                Case "Textbox"
            txtstream.WriteLine ("mystr = mystr & ""<td><input type=text
Value='" & rs.Fields(x).Value & "'></input></td>""" & vbcrlf")
                Case "Textarea"
            txtstream.WriteLine ("mystr = mystr & ""<td><textarea>" &
rs.Fields(x).Value & "</textarea></td>""" & vbcrlf")

            End Select

            rs.MoveNext

        Loop

        txtstream.WriteLine ("mystr = mystr & ""</tr>""" & vbcrlf")

    Next


    End Select


    End If

    txtstream.WriteLine ("mystr = mystr & ""</table>""" & vbcrlf")
    txtstream.WriteLine ("document.WriteLn(mystr)")
    txtstream.WriteLine ("")
    txtstream.WriteLine ("End Sub")
    txtstream.WriteLine ("")
    txtstream.WriteLine (Chr(60) & "/script>")
    txtstream.WriteLine ("</body>")
    txtstream.WriteLine ("</html>")
    txtstream.Close


    tempstr = ""
    Set txtstream = fso.OpenTextFile(ws.CurrentDirectory & "\" & Tablename &
".html", 1, True, -2)
        Do While txtstream.AtEndOfStream = False
            tempstr = tempstr & txtstream.ReadLine()
```

```
            tempstr = tempstr & vbCrLf
        Loop
        txtstream.Close
        textarea1.innerText = tempstr

End Sub

Sub Do_Bound()

    Select Case EngineConfiguration


        Case "cncmdrs"


            Set cn = CreateObject("ADODB.Connection")
            Set cmd = CreateObject("ADODB.Command")
            Set rs = CreateObject("ADODB.Recordset")


            cn.ConnectionString = "Provider=" & provider & ";Data Source=" &
fName.Value & ";"
            Call cn.Open()

            cmd.ActiveConnection = cn
            cmd.CommandType = 8
            cmd.CommandText = strQuery
            Call cmd.Execute()

            rs.CursorLocation = 3
            rs.LockType = 3
            Call rs.Open(cmd)


        Case "cnrs"

            Set cn = CreateObject("ADODB.Connection")
            Set rs = CreateObject("ADODB.Recordset")
```

```
            cn.ConnectionString = "Provider=" & Provider & ";Data Source=" &
fName.Value & ";"
            Call cn.Open()

            rs.ActiveConnection = cn
            rs.CursorLocation = 3
            rs.LockType = 3
            rs.Source = strQuery
            Call rs.Open()

        Case "cmdrs"

            Set cmd = CreateObject("ADODB.Command")
            Set rs = CreateObject("ADODB.Recordset")

            cmd.ActiveConnection = "Provider=" & Provider & ";Data Source=" &
fName.Value & ";"
            cmd.CommandType = 8
            cmd.CommandText = strQuery
            Call cmd.Execute()

            rs.CursorLocation = 3
            rs.LockType = 3
            Call rs.Open(cmd)

        Case "rs"

            Set rs = CreateObject("ADODB.Recordset")
            rs.ActiveConnection = "Provider=" & Provider & ";Data Source=" &
fName.Value & ";"
            rs.LockType = 3
            rs.Cursorlocation = 3
            rs.Source = strQuery
            Call rs.Open()

        End Select

        Set ws = CreateObject("WScript.Shell")
        Set fso = CreateObject("Scripting.FileSystemObject")
```

```
        Set txtstream = fso.OpenTextFile(ws.CurrentDirectory & "\" & Tablename &
".html", 2, True, -2)
        txtstream.WriteLine ("<html>")
        txtstream.WriteLine ("<head>")
        txtstream.WriteLine ("<title>" & Tablename & "</title>")


    Add_The_StyleSheet


    Select Case HTMLEngineConfiguration


        Case "cncmdrs"


            txtstream.WriteLine ("<object id=""cmd"" CLASSID=""clsid:00000507-
0000-0010-8000-00AA006D2EA4"" height=""0"" width=""0""></object>")
            txtstream.WriteLine ("<object id=""cn"" CLASSID=""clsid:00000514-
0000-0010-8000-00AA006D2EA4"" height=""0"" width=""0""></object>")
            txtstream.WriteLine ("<object id=""rs"" CLASSID=""clsid:00000535-
0000-0010-8000-00AA006D2EA4"" height=""0"" width=""0""></object>")
            txtstream.WriteLine ("</head>")
            txtstream.WriteLine ("<body>")
            txtstream.WriteLine ("<script language='vbscript'>")
            txtstream.WriteLine ("")
            txtstream.WriteLine ("cn.ConnectionString = ""Provider=" & Provider &
";Data Source=" & fName.Value & ";"" ")
            txtstream.WriteLine ("Call cn.Open()")
            txtstream.WriteLine ("")
            txtstream.WriteLine ("cmd.ActiveConnection = cn")
            txtstream.WriteLine ("cmd.CommandType = 8")
            txtstream.WriteLine ("cmd.CommandText = """ & strQuery & """ ")
            txtstream.WriteLine ("Call cmd.Execute()")
            txtstream.WriteLine ("")
            txtstream.WriteLine ("rs.CursorLocation = 3")
            txtstream.WriteLine ("rs.LockType = 3")
            txtstream.WriteLine ("Call rs.Open(cmd)")
            txtstream.WriteLine ("")
            txtstream.WriteLine (Chr(60) & "/script>")
```

```vbscript
Case "cnrs"

       txtstream.WriteLine ("<object id="""cn""" CLASSID="""clsid:00000514-0000-
0010-8000-00AA006D2EA4""" height="""0""" width="""0"""></object>")
       txtstream.WriteLine ("<object id="""rs""" CLASSID="""clsid:00000535-0000-
0010-8000-00AA006D2EA4""" height="""0""" width="""0"""></object>")
       txtstream.WriteLine ("</head>")
       txtstream.WriteLine ("<body>")
       txtstream.WriteLine ("<script language='vbscript'>")
       txtstream.WriteLine ("")
       txtstream.WriteLine ("cn.ConnectionString = """Provider=" & Provider &
";Data Source=" & fName.Value & ";""" ")
       txtstream.WriteLine ("Call cn.Open()")
       txtstream.WriteLine ("")
       txtstream.WriteLine ("rs.ActiveConnection = cn")
       txtstream.WriteLine ("rs.CursorLocation = 3")
       txtstream.WriteLine ("rs.LockType = 3")
       txtstream.WriteLine ("rs.Source = """" & strQuery & """" ")
       txtstream.WriteLine ("Call rs.Open()")
       txtstream.WriteLine ("")
       txtstream.WriteLine (Chr(60) & "/script>")




Case "cmdrs"

       txtstream.WriteLine ("<object id="""cmd""" CLASSID="""clsid:00000507-
0000-0010-8000-00AA006D2EA4""" height="""0""" width="""0"""></object>")
       txtstream.WriteLine ("<object id="""rs""" CLASSID="""clsid:00000535-
0000-0010-8000-00AA006D2EA4""" height="""0""" width="""0"""></object>")
       txtstream.WriteLine ("</head>")
       txtstream.WriteLine ("<body>")
       txtstream.WriteLine ("<script language='vbscript'>")
       txtstream.WriteLine ("")
       txtstream.WriteLine ("cmd.ActiveConnection = """Provider=" & Provider &
";Data Source=" & fName.Value & ";""" ")
       txtstream.WriteLine ("cmd.CommandType = 8")
       txtstream.WriteLine ("cmd.CommandText = """" & strQuery & """" ")
       txtstream.WriteLine ("Call cmd.Execute()")
```

```
        txtstream.WriteLine ("")
        txtstream.WriteLine ("rs.CursorLocation = 3")
        txtstream.WriteLine ("rs.LockType = 3")
        txtstream.WriteLine ("Call rs.Open(cmd)")
        txtstream.WriteLine ("")
        txtstream.WriteLine (Chr(60) & "/script>")

    Case "rs"



        txtstream.WriteLine ("<object id=""rs"" CLASSID=""clsid:00000535-0000-
0010-8000-00AA006D2EA4"" height=""0"" width=""0""></object>")
        txtstream.WriteLine ("</head>")
        txtstream.WriteLine ("<body>")
        txtstream.WriteLine ("<script language='vbscript'>")
        txtstream.WriteLine ("")
        txtstream.WriteLine ("rs.ActiveConnection = ""Provider=" & Provider &
";Data Source=" & fName.Value & ";"" ")
        txtstream.WriteLine ("rs.LockType = 3")
        txtstream.WriteLine ("rs.Cursorlocation = 3")
        txtstream.WriteLine ("rs.Source = """ & strQuery & """ ")
        txtstream.WriteLine ("Call rs.Open()")
        txtstream.WriteLine ("")
        txtstream.WriteLine (Chr(60) & "/script>")

    End Select


        If StyleSheet = "InLine" Then


            Select Case Orientation


                Case "Single-Line Horizontal"

                    Select Case TableType

                        Case "Table"
```

```
            txtstream.WriteLine    ("<table    Border='1'    cellpadding='1'
cellspacing='1'>")

        Case "Report"

            txtstream.WriteLine    ("<table    Border='0'    cellpadding='1'
cellspacing='1'>")

    End Select

        txtstream.WriteLine ("<tr>")
        For x = 0 To rs.Fields.Count - 1

            txtstream.WriteLine    ("<th    style='font-family:Calibri,    Sans-
Serif;font-size: 12px;color:darkred;'>" & rs.Fields(x).Name & "</th>")

        Next
        txtstream.WriteLine ("</tr>")
        txtstream.WriteLine ("<tr>")
        For x = 0 To rs.Fields.Count - 1

        Select Case ControlType

            Case "Button"
        txtstream.WriteLine ("<td style='font-family:Calibri, Sans-Serif;font-
size:  12px;color:navy;'><input    type=button    datasrc=#rs    datafld='"    &
rs.Fields(x).Name & "'></input></td>")
            Case "Combobox"
        txtstream.WriteLine ("<td style='font-family:Calibri, Sans-Serif;font-
size:  12px;color:navy;'><select  datasrc=#rs  datafld='"  &  rs.Fields(x).Name  &
"'></select></td>")
            Case "Div"
        txtstream.WriteLine ("<td style='font-family:Calibri, Sans-Serif;font-
size:  12px;color:navy;'><div   datasrc=#rs   datafld='"   &   rs.Fields(x).Name   &
"'></div></td>")
            Case "Listbox"
```

```
            txtstream.WriteLine ("<td style='font-family:Calibri, Sans-Serif;font-
size:  12px;color:navy;'><select    multiple=true    datasrc=#rs    datafld='"    &
rs.Fields(x).Name & "'></option></select></td>")
                Case "Span"
            txtstream.WriteLine ("<td style='font-family:Calibri, Sans-Serif;font-
size:  12px;color:navy;'><span  datasrc=#rs  datafld='"  &  rs.Fields(x).Name  &
"'></span></td>")
                Case "Textbox"
            txtstream.WriteLine ("<td style='font-family:Calibri, Sans-Serif;font-
size: 12px;color:navy;'><input type=text datasrc=#rs datafld='" & rs.Fields(x).Name
& "'></input></td>")
                Case "Textarea"
            txtstream.WriteLine ("<td style='font-family:Calibri, Sans-Serif;font-
size:  12px;color:navy;'><textarea  datasrc=#rs  datafld='"  &  rs.Fields(x).Name  &
"'></textarea></td>")

                End Select

            Next

            txtstream.WriteLine ("</tr>")


        Case "Multi-Line Horizontal"


            Select Case TableType

                Case "Table"

                    txtstream.WriteLine    ("<table    Border='1'    cellpadding='1'
cellspacing='1' datasrc=#rs>")

                Case "Report"

                    txtstream.WriteLine    ("<table    Border='0'    cellpadding='1'
cellspacing='1' datasrc=#rs>")

                End Select
```

```
txtstream.WriteLine ("<thead><tr>")
For x = 0 To rs.Fields.Count - 1

    txtstream.WriteLine ("<th style='font-family:Calibri, Sans-
Serif;font-size: 12px;color:darkred;'>" & rs.Fields(x).Name & "</th>")

Next
txtstream.WriteLine ("</tr></thead>")
txtstream.WriteLine ("<tbody><tr>")
For x = 0 To rs.Fields.Count - 1

Select Case ControlType

    Case "Button"
    txtstream.WriteLine ("<td style='font-family:Calibri, Sans-Serif;font-
size: 12px;color:navy;'><input type=button datasrc=#rs datafld='" &
rs.Fields(x).Name & "'></input></td>")
    Case "Combobox"
    txtstream.WriteLine ("<td style='font-family:Calibri, Sans-Serif;font-
size: 12px;color:navy;'><select datasrc=#rs datafld='" & rs.Fields(x).Name &
"'></select></td>")
    Case "Div"
    txtstream.WriteLine ("<td style='font-family:Calibri, Sans-Serif;font-
size: 12px;color:navy;'><div datasrc=#rs datafld='" & rs.Fields(x).Name &
"'></div></td>")
    Case "Listbox"
    txtstream.WriteLine ("<td style='font-family:Calibri, Sans-Serif;font-
size: 12px;color:navy;'><select multiple=true datasrc=#rs datafld='" &
rs.Fields(x).Name & "'></option></select></td>")
    Case "Span"
    txtstream.WriteLine ("<td style='font-family:Calibri, Sans-Serif;font-
size: 12px;color:navy;'><span datasrc=#rs datafld='" & rs.Fields(x).Name &
"'></span></td>")
    Case "Textbox"
    txtstream.WriteLine ("<td style='font-family:Calibri, Sans-Serif;font-
size: 12px;color:navy;'><input type=text datasrc=#rs datafld='" & rs.Fields(x).Name
& "'></input></td>")
    Case "Textarea"
```

```
            txtstream.WriteLine ("<td style='font-family:Calibri, Sans-Serif;font-
size: 12px;color:navy;'><textarea datasrc=#rs datafld='" & rs.Fields(x).Name &
"'></textarea></td>")

            End Select

        Next

        txtstream.WriteLine ("</tr></tbody>")


        Case "Single-Line Vertical"

            Select Case TableType

                Case "Table"

                    txtstream.WriteLine ("<table    Border='1'    cellpadding='1'
cellspacing='1'>")

                Case "Report"

                    txtstream.WriteLine ("<table    Border='0'    cellpadding='1'
cellspacing='1'>")

            End Select

            For x = 0 To rs.Fields.Count - 1

            Select Case ControlType

                Case "Button"
                    txtstream.WriteLine ("<td style='font-family:Calibri, Sans-Serif;font-
size:  12px;color:navy;'><input    type=button    datasrc=#rs    datafld='"    &
rs.Fields(x).Name & "'></input></td>")
                Case "Combobox"
```

```
            txtstream.WriteLine ("<td style='font-family:Calibri, Sans-Serif;font-
size: 12px;color:navy;'><select datasrc=#rs datafld='" & rs.Fields(x).Name &
"'></select></td>")
                    Case "Div"
            txtstream.WriteLine ("<td style='font-family:Calibri, Sans-Serif;font-
size: 12px;color:navy;'><div datasrc=#rs datafld='" & rs.Fields(x).Name &
"'></div></td>")
                    Case "Listbox"
            txtstream.WriteLine ("<td style='font-family:Calibri, Sans-Serif;font-
size:    12px;color:navy;'><select    multiple=true    datasrc=#rs    datafld='"    &
rs.Fields(x).Name & "'></option></select></td>")
                    Case "Span"
            txtstream.WriteLine ("<td style='font-family:Calibri, Sans-Serif;font-
size: 12px;color:navy;'><span datasrc=#rs datafld='" & rs.Fields(x).Name &
"'></span></td>")
                    Case "Textbox"
            txtstream.WriteLine ("<td style='font-family:Calibri, Sans-Serif;font-
size: 12px;color:navy;'><input type=text datasrc=#rs datafld='" & rs.Fields(x).Name
& "'></input></td>")
                    Case "Textarea"
            txtstream.WriteLine ("<td style='font-family:Calibri, Sans-Serif;font-
size: 12px;color:navy;'><textarea datasrc=#rs datafld='" & rs.Fields(x).Name &
"'></textarea></td>")


            End Select

        Next


        End Select

    Else

    Select Case Orientation

        Case "Single-Line Horizontal"

        Select Case TableType
```

```vb
        Case "Table"

            txtstream.WriteLine      ("<table     Border='1'    cellpadding='1'
cellspacing='1'>")

        Case "Report"

            txtstream.WriteLine      ("<table     Border='0'    cellpadding='1'
cellspacing='1'>")

    End Select


    txtstream.WriteLine ("<tr>")
    For x = 0 To rs.Fields.Count - 1

        txtstream.WriteLine ("<th >" & rs.Fields(x).Name & "</th>")

    Next
    txtstream.WriteLine ("</tr>")
    txtstream.WriteLine ("<tr>")
    For x = 0 To rs.Fields.Count - 1

        Select Case ControlType

            Case "Button"
        txtstream.WriteLine ("<td ><input type=button datasrc=#rs datafld='"
& rs.Fields(x).Name & "'></input></td>")
            Case "Combobox"
        txtstream.WriteLine   ("<td   ><select   datasrc=#rs   datafld='"   &
rs.Fields(x).Name & "'></select></td>")
            Case "Div"
        txtstream.WriteLine   ("<td    ><div    datasrc=#rs    datafld='"    &
rs.Fields(x).Name & "'></div></td>")
            Case "Listbox"
        txtstream.WriteLine   ("<td   ><select   multiple=true   datasrc=#rs
datafld='" & rs.Fields(x).Name & "'></option></select></td>")
            Case "Span"
        txtstream.WriteLine   ("<td    ><span    datasrc=#rs    datafld='"    &
rs.Fields(x).Name & "'></span></td>")
```

```
            Case "Textbox"
                txtstream.WriteLine ("<td ><input type=text datasrc=#rs datafld='" &
rs.Fields(x).Name & "'></input></td>")
            Case "Textarea"
                txtstream.WriteLine ("<td ><textarea datasrc=#rs datafld='" &
rs.Fields(x).Name & "'></textarea></td>")

        End Select


        Next

        txtstream.WriteLine ("</tr>")


    Case "Multi-Line Horizontal"


        Select Case TableType

            Case "Table"

                txtstream.WriteLine ("<table Border='1' cellpadding='1'
cellspacing='1' datasrc=#rs>")

            Case "Report"

                txtstream.WriteLine ("<table Border='0' cellpadding='1'
cellspacing='1' datasrc=#rs>")

        End Select

        txtstream.WriteLine ("<thead><tr>")
        For x = 0 To rs.Fields.Count - 1

            txtstream.WriteLine ("<th >" & rs.Fields(x).Name & "</th>")

        Next
        txtstream.WriteLine ("</tr></thead>")
```

```
txtstream.WriteLine ("<tbody><tr>")
For x = 0 To rs.Fields.Count - 1

    Select Case ControlType

        Case "Button"
    txtstream.WriteLine ("<td ><input type=button datasrc=#rs datafld='"
& rs.Fields(x).Name & "'></input></td>")
        Case "Combobox"
    txtstream.WriteLine ("<td ><select datasrc=#rs datafld='" &
rs.Fields(x).Name & "'></select></td>")
        Case "Div"
    txtstream.WriteLine ("<td ><div datasrc=#rs datafld='" &
rs.Fields(x).Name & "'></div></td>")
        Case "Listbox"
    txtstream.WriteLine ("<td ><select multiple=true datasrc=#rs
datafld='" & rs.Fields(x).Name & "'></option></select></td>")
        Case "Span"
    txtstream.WriteLine ("<td ><span datasrc=#rs datafld='" &
rs.Fields(x).Name & "'></span></td>")
        Case "Textbox"
    txtstream.WriteLine ("<td ><input type=text datasrc=#rs datafld='" &
rs.Fields(x).Name & "'></input></td>")
        Case "Textarea"
    txtstream.WriteLine ("<td ><textarea datasrc=#rs datafld='" &
rs.Fields(x).Name & "'></textarea></td>")

    End Select

Next

    txtstream.WriteLine ("</tr></tbody>")



Case "Single-Line Vertical"


Select Case TableType
```

```
                Case "Table"

                        txtstream.WriteLine    ("<table    Border='1'    cellpadding='1'
cellspacing='1'>")

                Case "Report"

                        txtstream.WriteLine    ("<table    Border='0'    cellpadding='1'
cellspacing='1'>")

            End Select

            For x = 0 To rs.Fields.Count - 1

            Select Case ControlType

                Case "Button"
            txtstream.WriteLine ("<td ><input type=button datasrc=#rs datafld='"
& rs.Fields(x).Name & "'></input></td>")
                Case "Combobox"
            txtstream.WriteLine    ("<td    ><select    datasrc=#rs    datafld='"    &
rs.Fields(x).Name & "'></select></td>")
                Case "Div"
            txtstream.WriteLine    ("<td    ><div    datasrc=#rs    datafld='"    &
rs.Fields(x).Name & "'></div></td>")
                Case "Listbox"
            txtstream.WriteLine    ("<td    ><select    multiple=true    datasrc=#rs
datafld='" & rs.Fields(x).Name & "'></option></select></td>")
                Case "Span"
            txtstream.WriteLine    ("<td    ><span    datasrc=#rs    datafld='"    &
rs.Fields(x).Name & "'></span></td>")
                Case "Textbox"
            txtstream.WriteLine ("<td ><input type=text datasrc=#rs datafld='" &
rs.Fields(x).Name & "'></input></td>")
                Case "Textarea"
            txtstream.WriteLine    ("<td    ><textarea    datasrc=#rs    datafld='"    &
rs.Fields(x).Name & "'></textarea></td>")

            End Select
```

```
                Next

            End Select


        End If

        txtstream.WriteLine ("</table>")
        txtstream.WriteLine ("</body>")
        txtstream.WriteLine ("</html>")
        txtstream.Close




        tempstr = ""
        Set txtstream = fso.OpenTextFile(ws.CurrentDirectory & "\" & Tablename &
".html", 1, True, -2)
        Do While txtstream.AtEndOfStream = False
           tempstr = tempstr & txtstream.ReadLine()
           tempstr = tempstr & vbCrLf
        Loop
        txtstream.Close
        textarea1.innerText = tempstr


    End Sub

  Sub LT1_OnClick()

    If fName.Value = "" then
        msgbox("Please provide the location and name of the database you want to
use before clicking here.")
        exit sub
    else
       cnstr = "Provider=" & Provider & ";Data Source = " & FName.Value & ";"

       Set cn = CreateObject("ADODB.Connection")
```

```
On Error Resume Next
cn.ConnectionString = cnstr
Call cn.Open()
if err.number = 0 then
    Set ws = CreateObject("WScript.Shell")
    Set fso = CreateObject("Scripting.FileSystemObject")
    Set txtstream = fso.OpenTextFile(ws.CurrentDirectory & "\tables.txt", 2,
true, -2)
    Set rs1 = cn.OpenSchema(20)
    Dim l()
    Redim l(3)
    l(0) = Len("Tablename")
    l(1) = Len("TableType")
    l(2) = Len("Description")

    Do While rs1.EOF = false
       if len(rs1.Fields("TABLE_NAME").Value) > l(0) then
          l(0) = len(rs1.Fields("TABLE_NAME").Value)
       End If

       if len(rs1.Fields("TABLE_TYPE").Value) > l(1) then
          l(1) = len(rs1.Fields("TABLE_TYPE").Value)
       End If

       if len(rs1.Fields("TABLE_DESCRIPTION").Value) > l(2) then
          l(2) = len(rs1.Fields("TABLE_DESCRIPTION").Value)
       End If

       rs1.MoveNext
    Loop

    rs1.MoveFirst

    l(0) = l(0) + 3
    l(1) = l(1) + 3
    l(2) = l(2) + 3

    Dim v

    v = l(0) - Len("Tablename")
```

```vbnet
mystr = "Tablename" & space(v)
v = l(1) - Len("TableType")
mystr = mystr & "TableType" & space(v)
v = l(2) - Len("Description")
mystr = mystr & "Description" & space(v)
txtstream.WriteLine(mystr)
mystr = ""
txtstream.WriteLine("")

Set tbl = document.GetElementByID("trex")
tbl.innerHTML = ""
Set opt = document.createElement("option")
opt.value = "*Select An Option*"
opt.text = "*Select An Option*"
opt.Selected = true
tbl.Options.Add(opt)



Do While rs1.EOF = false



   If mid(rs1.Fields("TABLE_NAME").Value, 1,4) <> "MSys" then

     If rs1.Fields("TABLE_TYPE").Value = "TABLE" then
       Set opt = document.createElement("option")
       opt.value = rs1.Fields("TABLE_NAME").Value
       opt.text = rs1.Fields("TABLE_NAME").Value
       tbl.Options.Add(opt)
     End If

         v = l(0) - Len(rs1.Fields("TABLE_NAME").Value)
         mystr = rs1.Fields("TABLE_NAME").Value & space(v)
         v = l(1) - Len(rs1.Fields("TABLE_TYPE").Value)
         mystr = mystr & rs1.Fields("TABLE_TYPE").Value & space(v)
         v = l(2) - Len(rs1.Fields("DESCRIPTION").Value)
         mystr = mystr & rs1.Fields("DESCRIPTION").Value
         txtstream.WriteLine(mystr)
         mystr = ""
```

```
            End If
            rs1.MoveNext
         Loop

         Dim tempstr
         tempstr = ""
         Set txtstream = fso.OpenTextFile(ws.CurrentDirectory & "\tables.txt", 1,
true, -2)
         Do While txtstream.AtEndOfStream = false
            tempstr = tempstr & txtstream.ReadLine()
            tempstr = tempstr & vbcrlf
         loop
         txtstream.Close
         textarea1.innerText = tempstr
      Else

         msgbox("Test connection Failed with: " & err.Description)

      End IF

   End If

   strQuery = ""

End Sub

Sub TestConnection1_OnClick()

   If fName.Value = "" then
      msgbox("Please provide the location and name of the database you want to
use before clicking here.")
      exit sub
   else
      cnstr = "Provider=" & Provider & ";Data Source = " & FName.Value & ";"
      Set cn = CreateObject("ADODB.Connection")
      On Error Resume Next
      cn.ConnectionString = cnstr
      Call cn.Open()
      if err.number = 0 then
         msgbox("Test connection succeeded.")
```

```vbnet
        else
           msgbox("Connecion failed with: " & err.Description)
        End If
     End If

   End Sub

   Sub Search_OnClick()

     Set ws = CreateObject("WScript.Shell")
     Set OpenDialog1 = CreateObject("MSComDlg.CommonDialog")

     With OpenDialog1
       .DialogTitle = "Open Database"
       .InitDir = ws.CurrentDirectory
       .Filter = "Microsoft Older Access Database(*.mdb)|*.mdb|Microsoft Newer
Access Database(*.accdb)|*.accdb"
       .FilterIndex = 2
       .MaxFileSize =32000
       .Flags = 2621952
       .ShowOpen
     End With
     If OpenDialog1.Filename <> "" then
        FName.Value = OpenDialog1.Filename
     End If

   End Sub

   Sub DataLinks1_OnClick()

   Set cn = createObject("ADODB.Connection")
   Set dl = CreateObject("Datalinks")
   Set cn = dl.PromptNew()
   Provider= cn.Provider
   cnstr = cn.ConnectionString
   FName.Value = cn.Properties("Data Source").Value

   End Sub

   Sub Clipboard1_OnClick()
```

```vbscript
    Set range = Textarea1.createTextRange()
    call range.findText(Textarea1.InnerText)
    range.select
    Call document.execCommand("Copy")
    Call document.execCommand("Unselect")

End Sub

Sub RunMe_OnClick()

    Set ws = CreateObject("WScript.Shell")
    Set fso = CreateObject("Scripting.FileSystemObject")

    Set txtstream = fso.OpenTextFile(ws.CurrentDirectory & "\" & Tablename &
".vbs", 2, true, -2)
    txtstream.WriteLine(Textarea1.innerText)
    txtstream.Close()
    Set txtstream = nothing
    Dim shorty
    Shorty = fso.GetFolder(ws.CurrentDirectory).ShortPath
    call ws.Run("C:\Windows\SysWOW64\wscript.exe " & Shorty & "\Code.vbs")
    Set fso = nothing

End Sub

Sub ViewMe_OnClick()

    Set ws = CreateObject("WScript.Shell")
    Set fso = CreateObject("Scripting.FileSystemObject")
    Dim shorty
    Shorty = fso.GetFolder(ws.CurrentDirectory).ShortPath
    Set txtstream = fso.OpenTextFile(shorty & "\" & Tablename & ".hta", 2, true, -
2)
    txtstream.WriteLine(Textarea1.innerText)
    txtstream.Close()
    call ws.Run(Shorty & "\" & Tablename & ".hta")
    Set fso = nothing
    Set ws = nothing
```

```
End Sub

Sub Document_OnClick()

End Sub

Sub wd_OnClick()

   Dim oWord
   Set range = Textarea1.createTextRange()
   Call range.findText(Textarea1.InnerText)
   range.Select
   Call Document.execCommand("Copy")
   Set oWordApp = CreateObject("Word.Application")
   oWordApp.Visible = True
   oWordApp.Activate
   Set oWord = oWordApp.Documents.Add()
   Set oParagraph = oWord.Application.ActiveDocument.Paragraphs.Add()
   oParagraph.Alignment = wdAlignParagraphJustify
   oParagraph.range.Font.Name = "Merriweather"
   oParagraph.range.Font.Size = 8
   oParagraph.CharacterUnitFirstLineIndent = 0.3
   oParagraph.Format.LineSpacing = 1.5
   oParagraph.Format.LineUnitBefore = 0
   oParagraph.Format.LineUnitAfter = 0
   oParagraph.range.PasteAndFormat (22)
   Call Document.execCommand("Unselect")

End Sub

Sub EMail_OnClick()

   if sn.Value = "" Then
      msgbox("Please enter the name of the mail server you want to connect to
before clicking here.")
      Exit Sub
   End If

   if lnu.Value = "" Then
```

```
        msgbox("Please enter your Logon name you use to log into mail server to
before clicking here.")
        Exit Sub
    End If

    if lpwd.Value = "" Then
        msgbox("Please enter your Logon password you use to log into mail server to
before clicking here.")
        Exit Sub
    End If

    if emfn.Value = "" Then
        msgbox("Please enter the user friendly name you use send and receive mail
before clicking here.")
        Exit Sub
    End If

    if ema.Value = "" Then
        msgbox("Please enter your email address you use send and receive mail before
clicking here.")
        Exit Sub
    End If

    if rec.Value = "" Then
        msgbox("Please enter the email address of the person you want to send this
mail to before clicking here.")
        Exit Sub
    End If

    if s.Value = "" Then
        msgbox("Please enter a subject or title you want to use with this mail before
clicking here.")
        Exit Sub
    End If


    Dim SMTPServer
    Dim SMTPLogon
    Dim LogonUserName
    Dim LogonPassword
```

```
    Dim strHTML
    Dim shorty
    Set ws = CreateObject("WScript.Shell")
    Set fso = CreateObject("Scripting.FileSystemObject")
    Shorty = fso.GetFolder(ws.CurrentDirectory).ShortPath
    Set txtstream = fso.OpenTextFile(shorty & "\" & Tablename & ".hta", 1, true, -
2)
    Do While txtstream.AtEndOfStream = false
        strHTML = strHTML & txtstream.ReadLine()
        strHTML = strHTML & vbcrlf
    Loop
    txtstream.Close()


EMailFrom = ema.Value
EmailFromName = emfn.Value
EmailTo = rec.Value
SMTPServer = sn.Value
SMTPLogon = lnu.Value
SMTPPassword = lpwd.Value




    Const SMTPSSL = True
    Const SMTPPort = 465

    Const cdoSendUsingPickup = 1  'Send message using local SMTP service pickup
directory.
    Const cdoSendUsingPort = 2    'Send the message using SMTP over TCP/IP
networking.

    Const cdoAnonymous = 0        ' No authentication
    Const cdoBasic = 1       ' BASIC clear text authentication
    Const cdoNTLM = 2        ' NTLM, Microsoft proprietary authentication

    ' First, create the message

    Set objMessage = CreateObject("CDO.Message")
    objMessage.Subject = s.Value
    objMessage.From = """" & EmailFromName & """ <" & EmailFrom & ">"
```

```
objMessage.To = EmailTo
objMessage.HTMLBody = strHTML

' Second, configure the server

objMessage.Configuration.Fields.Item("http://schemas.microsoft.com/cdo/config
uration/sendusing") = 2
objMessage.Configuration.Fields.Item("http://schemas.microsoft.com/cdo/config
uration/smtpusessl") = true
objMessage.Configuration.Fields.Item("http://schemas.microsoft.com/cdo/config
uration/smtpserver") = SMTPServer
objMessage.Configuration.Fields.Item("http://schemas.microsoft.com/cdo/config
uration/smtpauthenticate") = cdoBasic
objMessage.Configuration.Fields.Item("http://schemas.microsoft.com/cdo/config
uration/sendusername") = SMTPLogon
objMessage.Configuration.Fields.Item("http://schemas.microsoft.com/cdo/config
uration/sendpassword") = SMTPPassword
objMessage.Configuration.Fields.Item("http://schemas.microsoft.com/cdo/config
uration/smtpserverport") = SMTPPort
objMessage.Configuration.Fields.Item("http://schemas.microsoft.com/cdo/config
uration/smtpconnectiontimeout") = 60
Call objMessage.Configuration.Fields.Update()

On Error Resume Next

Call objMessage.Send()

If err.Number = 0 then

    Msgbox("Your message has been sent successfully!")

else

    Msgbox("Unable to send the mail. Error Message: " & err.Description)

    err.Clear

End If

End Sub
```

```vbscript
Sub Providers_OnClick()

    Const HKEY_LOCAL_MACHINE = &H80000002
    strComputer = "."
    Dim strValue
    Set oReg = GetObject("winmgmts:{impersonationLevel=impersonate}!\\.\root\default:StdRegProv")
    oReg.EnumKey HKEY_LOCAL_MACHINE, "SOFTWARE\Wow6432Node\Classes\CLSID", SubKeyNames
    mystr = "Providers found in HKEY_LOCAL_MACHINE\SOFTWARE\Wow6432Node\Classes\CLSID" & vbCrLf
    For Each skn In SubKeyNames
        If oReg.GetStringValue(HKEY_LOCAL_MACHINE, "SOFTWARE\Wow6432Node\Classes\CLSID\" & skn & "\Ole Db Provider", "", strValue) = 0 Then
            oReg.GetStringValue HKEY_LOCAL_MACHINE, "SOFTWARE\Wow6432Node\Classes\CLSID\" & skn, "", strValue
            mystr = mystr & strValue & vbCrLf
        End If
    Next
    mystr = mystr & "" & vbCrLf
    Textarea1.innerText = mystr

End Sub

Sub Drivers_OnClick()

    const HKEY_LOCAL_MACHINE = &H80000002
    strComputer = "."
    Set oReg= GetObject("winmgmts:{impersonationLevel=impersonate}!\\.\root\default:StdRegProv")

    if oReg.EnumValues (HKEY_LOCAL_MACHINE, "SOFTWARE\Wow6432Node\ODBC\ODBCINST.INI\ODBC Drivers", SubKeyNames) = 0 Then
```

```vbscript
      mystr                    =                    "Drivers                found              in
HKEY_LOCAL_MACHINE\SOFTWARE\Wow6432Node\ODBC\ODBCINST.INI\ODBC
Drivers" & vbcrlf
      mystr = mystr & "" & vbcrlf
      for each skn in SubKeyNames
         mystr = mystr & skn & vbcrlf
      Next
      mystr = mystr & "" & vbcrlf
      Textarea1.innerText = mystr
   End If

   End Sub

   Sub ISAMS_OnClick()

   Dim tempstr
   Dim SubKeyNames

   const HKEY_LOCAL_MACHINE = &H80000002
   strComputer = "."
   Set                                                                      oreg=
GetObject("winmgmts:{impersonationLevel=impersonate}!\\.\root\default:StdRegPr
ov")
      if                              oreg.EnumKey(HKEY_LOCAL_MACHINE,
   "SOFTWARE\Wow6432Node\Microsoft\Jet 3.5\ISAM Formats", SubKeyNames) = 0
   then
      mystr         =         "Found      Jet      3.5        ISAMS          in
HKEY_LOCAL_MACHINE\Wow6432Node\Microsoft\Jet 3.5\ISAM Formats" & vbcrlf
      mystr = mystr & "" & vbcrlf
      for each skn in SubKeyNames
         mystr = mystr & skn & vbcrlf
      Next
      mystr = mystr & "" & vbcrlf
   End If

      if                              oreg.EnumKey(HKEY_LOCAL_MACHINE,
   "SOFTWARE\Wow6432Node\Microsoft\Jet 4.0\ISAM Formats", SubKeyNames) = 0
   then
      mystr      =      mystr      &      "Found    Jet    4.0      ISAMS      in
HKEY_LOCAL_MACHINE\Wow6432Node\Microsoft\Jet 4.0\ISAM Formats" & vbcrlf
```

```vba
      mystr = mystr & "" & vbcrlf
      for each skn in SubKeyNames
         mystr = mystr & skn & vbcrlf
      Next
       mystr = mystr & "" & vbcrlf
   End If


   if                           oReg.EnumKey(HKEY_LOCAL_MACHINE,
"SOFTWARE\Wow6432Node\Microsoft\Office\10.0\Access Connectivity Engine\ISAM
Formats", SubKeyNames) = 0 then
      mystr    =    mystr    &    "Found    ACE    10.0    ISAMS    in
SOFTWARE\Wow6432Node\Microsoft\Office\10.0\Access Connectivity Engine\ISAM
Formats" & vbcrlf
      mystr = mystr & "" & vbcrlf
      for each skn in SubKeyNames
         mystr = mystr & skn & vbcrlf
      Next
      mystr = mystr & "" & vbcrlf
   End If


   if                           oReg.EnumKey(HKEY_LOCAL_MACHINE,
"SOFTWARE\Wow6432Node\Microsoft\Office\12.0\Access Connectivity Engine\ISAM
Formats", SubKeyNames) = 0 then
      mystr    =    mystr    &    "Found    ACE    12.0    ISAMS    in
KEY_LOCAL_MACHHINE\SOFTWARE\Wow6432Node\Microsoft\Office\12.0\Access
Connectivity Engine\ISAM Formats" & vbcrlf
      mystr = mystr & "" & vbcrlf
      for each skn in SubKeyNames
         mystr = mystr & skn & vbcrlf
      Next
      mystr = mystr & "" & vbcrlf
   End If


   if                           oReg.EnumKey(HKEY_LOCAL_MACHINE,
"SOFTWARE\Wow6432Node\Microsoft\Office\14.0\Access Connectivity Engine\ISAM
Formats", SubKeyNames) = 0 then
      mystr    =    mystr    &    "Found    ACE    14.0    ISAMS    in
KEY_LOCAL_MACHHINE\SOFTWARE\Wow6432Node\Microsoft\Office\14.0\Access
Connectivity Engine\ISAM Formats" & vbcrlf
      mystr = mystr & "" & vbcrlf
```

```
        for each skn in SubKeyNames
            mystr = mystr & skn & vbcrlf
        Next
        mystr = mystr & "" & vbcrlf
    End If


    if                          oReg.EnumKey(HKEY_LOCAL_MACHINE,
    "SOFTWARE\Wow6432Node\Microsoft\Office\15.0\Access Connectivity Engine\ISAM
    Formats", SubKeyNames) = 0 then
        mystr   =   mystr   &   "Found   ACE   15.0   ISAMS   in
    KEY_LOCAL_MACHHINE\SOFTWARE\Wow6432Node\Microsoft\Office\15.0\Access
    Connectivity Engine\ISAM Formats" & vbcrlf
        mystr = mystr & "" & vbcrlf
        for each skn in SubKeyNames
            mystr = mystr & skn & vbcrlf
        Next
        mystr = mystr & "" & vbcrlf
    End If



    if                          oReg.EnumKey(HKEY_LOCAL_MACHINE,
    "SOFTWARE\Wow6432Node\Microsoft\Office\16.0\Access Connectivity Engine\ISAM
    Formats", SubKeyNames) = 0 then
        mystr   =   mystr   &   "Found   ACE   16.0   ISAMS   in
    KEY_LOCAL_MACHHINE\SOFTWARE\Wow6432Node\Microsoft\Office\16.0\Access
    Connectivity Engine\ISAM Formats" & vbcrlf
        mystr = mystr & "" & vbcrlf
        for each skn in SubKeyNames
            mystr = mystr & skn & vbcrlf
        Next
        mystr = mystr & "" & vbcrlf
    End If

    Textarea1.innerText = mystr

    End Sub

    Sub Create_Template()

    End Sub
```

```vba
Sub Add_The_StyleSheet()

    Select Case StyleSheet

        Case "None"

        Case "Basic"

            txtstream.WriteLine("<style type='text/css'>")
            txtstream.WriteLine("th")
            txtstream.WriteLine("{")
            txtstream.WriteLine("   COLOR: Darkred;")
            txtstream.WriteLine("}")
            txtstream.WriteLine("td")
            txtstream.WriteLine("{")
            txtstream.WriteLine("   COLOR: navy;")
            txtstream.WriteLine("}")
            txtstream.WriteLine("</style>")

        Case "InLine"


        Case "Table"

            txtstream.WriteLine("<style type=text/css>")
            txtstream.WriteLine("#itsthetable {")
            txtstream.WriteLine(" font-family:     Georgia,     """"""Times     New
Roman"""""", Times, serif;")
            txtstream.WriteLine(" color: #036;")
            txtstream.WriteLine("}")

            txtstream.WriteLine("caption {")
            txtstream.WriteLine(" font-size: 48px;")
            txtstream.WriteLine(" color: #036;")
            txtstream.WriteLine(" font-weight: bolder;")
            txtstream.WriteLine(" font-variant: small-caps;")
            txtstream.WriteLine("}")
```

```
txtstream.WriteLine("th {")
txtstream.WriteLine(" font-size: 12px;")
txtstream.WriteLine(" color: #FFF;")
txtstream.WriteLine(" background-color: #06C;")
txtstream.WriteLine(" padding: 8px 4px;")
txtstream.WriteLine(" border-bottom: 1px solid #015ebc;")
txtstream.WriteLine("}")

txtstream.WriteLine("table {")
txtstream.WriteLine(" margin: 0;")
txtstream.WriteLine(" padding: 0;")
txtstream.WriteLine(" border-collapse: collapse;")
txtstream.WriteLine(" border: 1px solid #06C;")
txtstream.WriteLine(" width: 100%")
txtstream.WriteLine("}")

txtstream.WriteLine("#itsthetable th a:link, #itsthetable th a:visited {")
txtstream.WriteLine(" color: #FFF;")
txtstream.WriteLine(" text-decoration: none;")
txtstream.WriteLine(" border-left: 5px solid #FFF;")
txtstream.WriteLine(" padding-left: 3px;")
txtstream.WriteLine("}")

txtstream.WriteLine("th a:hover, #itsthetable th a:active {")
txtstream.WriteLine(" color: #F90;")
txtstream.WriteLine(" text-decoration: line-through;")
txtstream.WriteLine(" border-left: 5px solid #F90;")
txtstream.WriteLine(" padding-left: 3px;")
txtstream.WriteLine("}")

txtstream.WriteLine("tbody th:hover {")
txtstream.WriteLine(" background-image: url(imgs/tbody_hover.gif);")
txtstream.WriteLine(" background-position: bottom;")
txtstream.WriteLine(" background-repeat: repeat-x;")
txtstream.WriteLine("}")

txtstream.WriteLine("td {")
txtstream.WriteLine(" background-color: #f2f2f2;")
```

```
txtstream.WriteLine(" padding: 4px;")
txtstream.WriteLine(" font-size: 12px;")
txtstream.WriteLine("}")

txtstream.WriteLine("#itsthetable td:hover {")
txtstream.WriteLine(" background-color: #f8f8f8;")

txtstream.WriteLine("}")

txtstream.WriteLine("#itsthetable td a:link, #itsthetable td a:visited {")
txtstream.WriteLine(" color: #039;")
txtstream.WriteLine(" text-decoration: none;")
txtstream.WriteLine(" border-left: 3px solid #039;")
txtstream.WriteLine(" padding-left: 3px;")
txtstream.WriteLine("}")

txtstream.WriteLine("#itsthetable td a:hover, #itsthetable td a:active {")
txtstream.WriteLine(" color: #06C;")
txtstream.WriteLine(" text-decoration: line-through;")
txtstream.WriteLine(" border-left: 3px solid #06C;")
txtstream.WriteLine(" padding-left: 3px;")
txtstream.WriteLine("}")

txtstream.WriteLine("#itsthetable th {")
txtstream.WriteLine(" text-align: left;")
txtstream.WriteLine(" width: 150px;")
txtstream.WriteLine("}")

txtstream.WriteLine("#itsthetable tr {")
txtstream.WriteLine(" border-bottom: 1px solid #CCC;")
txtstream.WriteLine("}")

txtstream.WriteLine("#itsthetable thead th {")
txtstream.WriteLine(" background-image: url(imgs/thead_back.gif);")
txtstream.WriteLine(" background-repeat: repeat-x;")
txtstream.WriteLine(" background-color: #06C;")
txtstream.WriteLine(" height: 30px;")
txtstream.WriteLine(" font-size: 18px;")
txtstream.WriteLine(" text-align: center;")
```

```
        txtstream.WriteLine(" text-shadow: #333 2px 2px;")
        txtstream.WriteLine(" border: 2px;")
        txtstream.WriteLine("}")

        txtstream.WriteLine("#itsthetable tfoot th {")
        txtstream.WriteLine(" background-image: url(imgs/tfoot_back.gif);")
        txtstream.WriteLine(" background-repeat: repeat-x;")
        txtstream.WriteLine(" background-color: #036;")
        txtstream.WriteLine(" height: 30px;")
        txtstream.WriteLine(" font-size: 28px;")
        txtstream.WriteLine(" text-align: center;")
        txtstream.WriteLine(" text-shadow: #333 2px 2px;")
        txtstream.WriteLine("}")

        txtstream.WriteLine("#itsthetable tfoot td {")
        txtstream.WriteLine(" background-image: url(imgs/tfoot_back.gif);")
        txtstream.WriteLine(" background-repeat: repeat-x;")
        txtstream.WriteLine(" background-color: #036;")
        txtstream.WriteLine(" color: FFF;")
        txtstream.WriteLine(" height: 30px;")
        txtstream.WriteLine(" font-size: 24px;")
        txtstream.WriteLine(" text-align: left;")
        txtstream.WriteLine(" text-shadow: #333 2px 2px;")
        txtstream.WriteLine("}")

        txtstream.WriteLine("tbody  td  a[href="""""http://www.csslab.cl/"""""]
{")

        txtstream.WriteLine(" font-weight: bolder;")
        txtstream.WriteLine("}")
        txtstream.WriteLine("</style>")


    Case "BlackAndWhiteText"


        txtstream.WriteLine("<style type='text/css'>")
        txtstream.WriteLine("th")
        txtstream.WriteLine("{")
        txtstream.WriteLine("   COLOR: white;")
        txtstream.WriteLine("   BACKGROUND-COLOR: black;")
```

```
txtstream.WriteLine("   FONT-FAMILY:font-family: Cambria, serif;")
txtstream.WriteLine("   FONT-SIZE: 12px;")
txtstream.WriteLine("   text-align: left;")
txtstream.WriteLine("   white-Space: nowrap;")
txtstream.WriteLine("}")
txtstream.WriteLine("td")
txtstream.WriteLine("{")
txtstream.WriteLine("   COLOR: white;")
txtstream.WriteLine("   BACKGROUND-COLOR: black;")
txtstream.WriteLine("   FONT-FAMILY: font-family: Cambria, serif;")
txtstream.WriteLine("   FONT-SIZE: 12px;")
txtstream.WriteLine("   text-align: left;")
txtstream.WriteLine("   white-Space: nowrap;")
txtstream.WriteLine("}")
txtstream.WriteLine("div")
txtstream.WriteLine("{")
txtstream.WriteLine("   COLOR: white;")
txtstream.WriteLine("   BACKGROUND-COLOR: black;")
txtstream.WriteLine("   FONT-FAMILY: font-family: Cambria, serif;")
txtstream.WriteLine("   FONT-SIZE: 10px;")
txtstream.WriteLine("   text-align: left;")
txtstream.WriteLine("   white-Space: nowrap;")
txtstream.WriteLine("}")
txtstream.WriteLine("span")
txtstream.WriteLine("{")
txtstream.WriteLine("   COLOR: white;")
txtstream.WriteLine("   BACKGROUND-COLOR: black;")
txtstream.WriteLine("   FONT-FAMILY: font-family: Cambria, serif;")
txtstream.WriteLine("   FONT-SIZE: 10px;")
txtstream.WriteLine("   text-align: left;")
txtstream.WriteLine("   white-Space: nowrap;")
txtstream.WriteLine("   display:inline-block;")
txtstream.WriteLine("   width: 100%;")
txtstream.WriteLine("}")
txtstream.WriteLine("textarea")
txtstream.WriteLine("{")
txtstream.WriteLine("   COLOR: white;")
txtstream.WriteLine("   BACKGROUND-COLOR: black;")
txtstream.WriteLine("   FONT-FAMILY: font-family: Cambria, serif;")
txtstream.WriteLine("   FONT-SIZE: 10px;")
```

```
txtstream.WriteLine("   text-align: left;")
txtstream.WriteLine("   white-Space: nowrap;")
txtstream.WriteLine("   width: 100%;")
txtstream.WriteLine("}")
txtstream.WriteLine("select")
txtstream.WriteLine("{")
txtstream.WriteLine("   COLOR: white;")
txtstream.WriteLine("   BACKGROUND-COLOR: black;")
txtstream.WriteLine("   FONT-FAMILY: font-family: Cambria, serif;")
txtstream.WriteLine("   FONT-SIZE: 10px;")
txtstream.WriteLine("   text-align: left;")
txtstream.WriteLine("   white-Space: nowrap;")
txtstream.WriteLine("   width: 100%;")
txtstream.WriteLine("}")
txtstream.WriteLine("input")
txtstream.WriteLine("{")
txtstream.WriteLine("   COLOR: white;")
txtstream.WriteLine("   BACKGROUND-COLOR: black;")
txtstream.WriteLine("   FONT-FAMILY: font-family: Cambria, serif;")
txtstream.WriteLine("   FONT-SIZE: 12px;")
txtstream.WriteLine("   text-align: left;")
txtstream.WriteLine("   display:table-cell;")
txtstream.WriteLine("   white-Space: nowrap;")
txtstream.WriteLine("}")
txtstream.WriteLine("h1 {")
txtstream.WriteLine("color: antiquewhite;")
txtstream.WriteLine("text-shadow: 1px 1px 1px black;")
txtstream.WriteLine("padding: 3px;")
txtstream.WriteLine("text-align: center;")
txtstream.WriteLine("box-shadow: in2px 2px 5px rgba(0,0,0,0.5), in-
2px -2px 5px rgba(255,255,255,0.5);")
txtstream.WriteLine("}")
txtstream.WriteLine("</style>")

   Case "ColoredText"

txtstream.WriteLine("<style type='text/css'>")
txtstream.WriteLine("th")
txtstream.WriteLine("{")
txtstream.WriteLine("   COLOR: darkred;")
```

```
txtstream.WriteLine("   BACKGROUND-COLOR: #eeeeee;")
txtstream.WriteLine("   FONT-FAMILY:font-family: Cambria, serif;")
txtstream.WriteLine("   FONT-SIZE: 12px;")
txtstream.WriteLine("   text-align: left;")
txtstream.WriteLine("   white-Space: nowrap;")
txtstream.WriteLine("}")
txtstream.WriteLine("td")
txtstream.WriteLine("{")
txtstream.WriteLine("   COLOR: navy;")
txtstream.WriteLine("   BACKGROUND-COLOR: #eeeeee;")
txtstream.WriteLine("   FONT-FAMILY: font-family: Cambria, serif;")
txtstream.WriteLine("   FONT-SIZE: 12px;")
txtstream.WriteLine("   text-align: left;")
txtstream.WriteLine("   white-Space: nowrap;")
txtstream.WriteLine("}")
txtstream.WriteLine("div")
txtstream.WriteLine("{")
txtstream.WriteLine("   COLOR: white;")
txtstream.WriteLine("   BACKGROUND-COLOR: navy;")
txtstream.WriteLine("   FONT-FAMILY: font-family: Cambria, serif;")
txtstream.WriteLine("   FONT-SIZE: 10px;")
txtstream.WriteLine("   text-align: left;")
txtstream.WriteLine("   white-Space: nowrap;")
txtstream.WriteLine("}")
txtstream.WriteLine("span")
txtstream.WriteLine("{")
txtstream.WriteLine("   COLOR: white;")
txtstream.WriteLine("   BACKGROUND-COLOR: navy;")
txtstream.WriteLine("   FONT-FAMILY: font-family: Cambria, serif;")
txtstream.WriteLine("   FONT-SIZE: 10px;")
txtstream.WriteLine("   text-align: left;")
txtstream.WriteLine("   white-Space: nowrap;")
txtstream.WriteLine("   display:inline-block;")
txtstream.WriteLine("   width: 100%;")
txtstream.WriteLine("}")
txtstream.WriteLine("textarea")
txtstream.WriteLine("{")
txtstream.WriteLine("   COLOR: white;")
txtstream.WriteLine("   BACKGROUND-COLOR: navy;")
txtstream.WriteLine("   FONT-FAMILY: font-family: Cambria, serif;")
```

```
                  txtstream.WriteLine("   FONT-SIZE: 10px;")
                  txtstream.WriteLine("   text-align: left;")
                  txtstream.WriteLine("   white-Space: nowrap;")
                  txtstream.WriteLine("   width: 100%;")
                  txtstream.WriteLine("}")
                  txtstream.WriteLine("select")
                  txtstream.WriteLine("{")
                  txtstream.WriteLine("   COLOR: white;")
                  txtstream.WriteLine("   BACKGROUND-COLOR: navy;")
                  txtstream.WriteLine("   FONT-FAMILY: font-family: Cambria, serif;")
                  txtstream.WriteLine("   FONT-SIZE: 10px;")
                  txtstream.WriteLine("   text-align: left;")
                  txtstream.WriteLine("   white-Space: nowrap;")
                  txtstream.WriteLine("   width: 100%;")
                  txtstream.WriteLine("}")
                  txtstream.WriteLine("input")
                  txtstream.WriteLine("{")
                  txtstream.WriteLine("   COLOR: white;")
                  txtstream.WriteLine("   BACKGROUND-COLOR: navy;")
                  txtstream.WriteLine("   FONT-FAMILY: font-family: Cambria, serif;")
                  txtstream.WriteLine("   FONT-SIZE: 12px;")
                  txtstream.WriteLine("   text-align: left;")
                  txtstream.WriteLine("   display:table-cell;")
                  txtstream.WriteLine("   white-Space: nowrap;")
                  txtstream.WriteLine("}")
                  txtstream.WriteLine("h1 {")
                  txtstream.WriteLine("color: antiquewhite;")
                  txtstream.WriteLine("text-shadow: 1px 1px 1px black;")
                  txtstream.WriteLine("padding: 3px;")
                  txtstream.WriteLine("text-align: center;")
                  txtstream.WriteLine("box-shadow: in2px 2px 5px rgba(0,0,0,0.5), in-
2px -2px 5px rgba(255,255,255,0.5);")
                  txtstream.WriteLine("}")
                  txtstream.WriteLine("</style>")


            Case "OscillatingRowColors"


                  txtstream.WriteLine("<style type='text/css'> ")
```

```
txtstream.WriteLine("th")
txtstream.WriteLine("{")
txtstream.WriteLine("    COLOR: white;")
txtstream.WriteLine("    BACKGROUND-COLOR: navy;")
txtstream.WriteLine("    FONT-FAMILY:font-family: Cambria, serif;")
txtstream.WriteLine("    FONT-SIZE: 12px;")
txtstream.WriteLine("    text-align: left;")
txtstream.WriteLine("    white-Space: nowrap;")
txtstream.WriteLine("}")
txtstream.WriteLine("td")
txtstream.WriteLine("{")
txtstream.WriteLine("    COLOR: navy;")
txtstream.WriteLine("    FONT-FAMILY: font-family: Cambria, serif;")
txtstream.WriteLine("    FONT-SIZE: 12px;")
txtstream.WriteLine("    text-align: left;")
txtstream.WriteLine("    white-Space: nowrap;")
txtstream.WriteLine("}")
txtstream.WriteLine("div")
txtstream.WriteLine("{")
txtstream.WriteLine("    COLOR: navy;")
txtstream.WriteLine("    FONT-FAMILY: font-family: Cambria, serif;")
txtstream.WriteLine("    FONT-SIZE: 12px;")
txtstream.WriteLine("    text-align: left;")
txtstream.WriteLine("    white-Space: nowrap;")
txtstream.WriteLine("}")
txtstream.WriteLine("span")
txtstream.WriteLine("{")
txtstream.WriteLine("    COLOR: navy;")
txtstream.WriteLine("    FONT-FAMILY: font-family: Cambria, serif;")
txtstream.WriteLine("    FONT-SIZE: 12px;")
txtstream.WriteLine("    text-align: left;")
txtstream.WriteLine("    white-Space: nowrap;")
txtstream.WriteLine("    width: 100%;")
txtstream.WriteLine("}")
txtstream.WriteLine("textarea")
txtstream.WriteLine("{")
txtstream.WriteLine("    COLOR: navy;")
txtstream.WriteLine("    FONT-FAMILY: font-family: Cambria, serif;")
txtstream.WriteLine("    FONT-SIZE: 12px;")
txtstream.WriteLine("    text-align: left;")
```

```
txtstream.WriteLine("    white-Space: nowrap;")
txtstream.WriteLine("    display:inline-block;")
txtstream.WriteLine("    width: 100%;")
txtstream.WriteLine("}")
txtstream.WriteLine("select")
txtstream.WriteLine("{")
txtstream.WriteLine("    COLOR: navy;")
txtstream.WriteLine("    FONT-FAMILY: font-family: Cambria, serif;")
txtstream.WriteLine("    FONT-SIZE: 10px;")
txtstream.WriteLine("    text-align: left;")
txtstream.WriteLine("    white-Space: nowrap;")
txtstream.WriteLine("    display:inline-block;")
txtstream.WriteLine("    width: 100%;")
txtstream.WriteLine("}")
txtstream.WriteLine("input")
txtstream.WriteLine("{")
txtstream.WriteLine("    COLOR: navy;")
txtstream.WriteLine("    FONT-FAMILY: font-family: Cambria, serif;")
txtstream.WriteLine("    FONT-SIZE: 12px;")
txtstream.WriteLine("    text-align: left;")
txtstream.WriteLine("    display:table-cell;")
txtstream.WriteLine("    white-Space: nowrap;")
txtstream.WriteLine("}")
txtstream.WriteLine("h1 {")
txtstream.WriteLine("color: antiquewhite;")
txtstream.WriteLine("text-shadow: 1px 1px 1px black;")
txtstream.WriteLine("padding: 3px;")
txtstream.WriteLine("text-align: center;")
txtstream.WriteLine("box-shadow: in2px 2px 5px rgba(0,0,0,0.5), in-
2px -2px 5px rgba(255,255,255,0.5);")
txtstream.WriteLine("}")
txtstream.WriteLine("tr:nth-child(even){background-color:#f2f2f2;}")
txtstream.WriteLine("tr:nth-child(odd){background-color:#cccccc;
color:#f2f2f2;}")
txtstream.WriteLine("</style>")

    Case "GhostDecorated"

    txtstream.WriteLine("<style type='text/css'>")
    txtstream.WriteLine("th")
```

```
txtstream.WriteLine("{")
txtstream.WriteLine("   COLOR: black;")
txtstream.WriteLine("   BACKGROUND-COLOR: white;")
txtstream.WriteLine("   FONT-FAMILY:font-family: Cambria, serif;")
txtstream.WriteLine("   FONT-SIZE: 12px;")
txtstream.WriteLine("   text-align: left;")
txtstream.WriteLine("   white-Space: nowrap;")
txtstream.WriteLine("}")
txtstream.WriteLine("td")
txtstream.WriteLine("{")
txtstream.WriteLine("   COLOR: black;")
txtstream.WriteLine("   BACKGROUND-COLOR: white;")
txtstream.WriteLine("   FONT-FAMILY: font-family: Cambria, serif;")
txtstream.WriteLine("   FONT-SIZE: 12px;")
txtstream.WriteLine("   text-align: left;")
txtstream.WriteLine("   white-Space: nowrap;")
txtstream.WriteLine("}")
txtstream.WriteLine("div")
txtstream.WriteLine("{")
txtstream.WriteLine("   COLOR: black;")
txtstream.WriteLine("   BACKGROUND-COLOR: white;")
txtstream.WriteLine("   FONT-FAMILY: font-family: Cambria, serif;")
txtstream.WriteLine("   FONT-SIZE: 10px;")
txtstream.WriteLine("   text-align: left;")
txtstream.WriteLine("   white-Space: nowrap;")
txtstream.WriteLine("}")
txtstream.WriteLine("span")
txtstream.WriteLine("{")
txtstream.WriteLine("   COLOR: black;")
txtstream.WriteLine("   BACKGROUND-COLOR: white;")
txtstream.WriteLine("   FONT-FAMILY: font-family: Cambria, serif;")
txtstream.WriteLine("   FONT-SIZE: 10px;")
txtstream.WriteLine("   text-align: left;")
txtstream.WriteLine("   white-Space: nowrap;")
txtstream.WriteLine("   display:inline-block;")
txtstream.WriteLine("   width: 100%;")
txtstream.WriteLine("}")
txtstream.WriteLine("textarea")
txtstream.WriteLine("{")
txtstream.WriteLine("   COLOR: black;")
```

```
txtstream.WriteLine("    BACKGROUND-COLOR: white;")
txtstream.WriteLine("    FONT-FAMILY: font-family: Cambria, serif;")
txtstream.WriteLine("    FONT-SIZE: 10px;")
txtstream.WriteLine("    text-align: left;")
txtstream.WriteLine("    white-Space: nowrap;")
txtstream.WriteLine("    width: 100%;")
txtstream.WriteLine("}")
txtstream.WriteLine("select")
txtstream.WriteLine("{")
txtstream.WriteLine("    COLOR: black;")
txtstream.WriteLine("    BACKGROUND-COLOR: white;")
txtstream.WriteLine("    FONT-FAMILY: font-family: Cambria, serif;")
txtstream.WriteLine("    FONT-SIZE: 10px;")
txtstream.WriteLine("    text-align: left;")
txtstream.WriteLine("    white-Space: nowrap;")
txtstream.WriteLine("    width: 100%;")
txtstream.WriteLine("}")
txtstream.WriteLine("input")
txtstream.WriteLine("{")
txtstream.WriteLine("    COLOR: black;")
txtstream.WriteLine("    BACKGROUND-COLOR: white;")
txtstream.WriteLine("    FONT-FAMILY: font-family: Cambria, serif;")
txtstream.WriteLine("    FONT-SIZE: 12px;")
txtstream.WriteLine("    text-align: left;")
txtstream.WriteLine("    display:table-cell;")
txtstream.WriteLine("    white-Space: nowrap;")
txtstream.WriteLine("}")
txtstream.WriteLine("h1 {")
txtstream.WriteLine("color: antiquewhite;")
txtstream.WriteLine("text-shadow: 1px 1px 1px black;")
txtstream.WriteLine("padding: 3px;")
txtstream.WriteLine("text-align: center;")
txtstream.WriteLine("box-shadow: in2px 2px 5px rgba(0,0,0,0.5), in-
2px -2px 5px rgba(255,255,255,0.5);")
txtstream.WriteLine("}")
txtstream.WriteLine("</style>")

        Case "3D"
```

```
txtstream.WriteLine("<style type='text/css'>")
txtstream.WriteLine("body")
txtstream.WriteLine("{")
txtstream.WriteLine("    PADDING-RIGHT: 0px;")
txtstream.WriteLine("    PADDING-LEFT: 0px;")
txtstream.WriteLine("    PADDING-BOTTOM: 0px;")
txtstream.WriteLine("    MARGIN: 0px;")
txtstream.WriteLine("    COLOR: #333;")
txtstream.WriteLine("    PADDING-TOP: 0px;")
txtstream.WriteLine("    FONT-FAMILY: verdana, arial, helvetica, sans-serif;")
txtstream.WriteLine("}")
txtstream.WriteLine("table")
txtstream.WriteLine("{")
txtstream.WriteLine("    BORDER-RIGHT: #999999 3px solid;")
txtstream.WriteLine("    PADDING-RIGHT: 6px;")
txtstream.WriteLine("    PADDING-LEFT: 6px;")
txtstream.WriteLine("    FONT-WEIGHT: Bold;")
txtstream.WriteLine("    FONT-SIZE: 14px;")
txtstream.WriteLine("    PADDING-BOTTOM: 6px;")
txtstream.WriteLine("    COLOR: Peru;")
txtstream.WriteLine("    LINE-HEIGHT: 14px;")
txtstream.WriteLine("    PADDING-TOP: 6px;")
txtstream.WriteLine("    BORDER-BOTTOM: #999 1px solid;")
txtstream.WriteLine("    BACKGROUND-COLOR: #eeeeee;")
txtstream.WriteLine("    FONT-FAMILY: verdana, arial, helvetica, sans-serif;")
txtstream.WriteLine("    FONT-SIZE: 12px;")
txtstream.WriteLine("}")
txtstream.WriteLine("th")
txtstream.WriteLine("{")
txtstream.WriteLine("    BORDER-RIGHT: #999999 3px solid;")
txtstream.WriteLine("    PADDING-RIGHT: 6px;")
txtstream.WriteLine("    PADDING-LEFT: 6px;")
txtstream.WriteLine("    FONT-WEIGHT: Bold;")
txtstream.WriteLine("    FONT-SIZE: 14px;")
txtstream.WriteLine("    PADDING-BOTTOM: 6px;")
txtstream.WriteLine("    COLOR: darkred;")
txtstream.WriteLine("    LINE-HEIGHT: 14px;")
txtstream.WriteLine("    PADDING-TOP: 6px;")
```

```
txtstream.WriteLine("    BORDER-BOTTOM: #999 1px solid;")
txtstream.WriteLine("    BACKGROUND-COLOR: #eeeeee;")
txtstream.WriteLine("    FONT-FAMILY:font-family: Cambria, serif;")
txtstream.WriteLine("    FONT-SIZE: 12px;")
txtstream.WriteLine("    text-align: left;")
txtstream.WriteLine("    white-Space: nowrap;")
txtstream.WriteLine("}")
txtstream.WriteLine(".th")
txtstream.WriteLine("{")
txtstream.WriteLine("    BORDER-RIGHT: #999999 2px solid;")
txtstream.WriteLine("    PADDING-RIGHT: 6px;")
txtstream.WriteLine("    PADDING-LEFT: 6px;")
txtstream.WriteLine("    FONT-WEIGHT: Bold;")
txtstream.WriteLine("    PADDING-BOTTOM: 6px;")
txtstream.WriteLine("    COLOR: black;")
txtstream.WriteLine("    PADDING-TOP: 6px;")
txtstream.WriteLine("    BORDER-BOTTOM: #999 2px solid;")
txtstream.WriteLine("    BACKGROUND-COLOR: #eeeeee;")
txtstream.WriteLine("    FONT-FAMILY: font-family: Cambria, serif;")
txtstream.WriteLine("    FONT-SIZE: 10px;")
txtstream.WriteLine("    text-align: right;")
txtstream.WriteLine("    white-Space: nowrap;")
txtstream.WriteLine("}")
txtstream.WriteLine("td")
txtstream.WriteLine("{")
txtstream.WriteLine("    BORDER-RIGHT: #999999 3px solid;")
txtstream.WriteLine("    PADDING-RIGHT: 6px;")
txtstream.WriteLine("    PADDING-LEFT: 6px;")
txtstream.WriteLine("    FONT-WEIGHT: Normal;")
txtstream.WriteLine("    PADDING-BOTTOM: 6px;")
txtstream.WriteLine("    COLOR: navy;")
txtstream.WriteLine("    LINE-HEIGHT: 14px;")
txtstream.WriteLine("    PADDING-TOP: 6px;")
txtstream.WriteLine("    BORDER-BOTTOM: #999 1px solid;")
txtstream.WriteLine("    BACKGROUND-COLOR: #eeeeee;")
txtstream.WriteLine("    FONT-FAMILY: font-family: Cambria, serif;")
txtstream.WriteLine("    FONT-SIZE: 12px;")
txtstream.WriteLine("    text-align: left;")
txtstream.WriteLine("    white-Space: nowrap;")
txtstream.WriteLine("}")
```

```
txtstream.WriteLine("div")
txtstream.WriteLine("{")
txtstream.WriteLine("    BORDER-RIGHT: #999999 3px solid;")
txtstream.WriteLine("    PADDING-RIGHT: 6px;")
txtstream.WriteLine("    PADDING-LEFT: 6px;")
txtstream.WriteLine("    FONT-WEIGHT: Normal;")
txtstream.WriteLine("    PADDING-BOTTOM: 6px;")
txtstream.WriteLine("    COLOR: white;")
txtstream.WriteLine("    PADDING-TOP: 6px;")
txtstream.WriteLine("    BORDER-BOTTOM: #999 1px solid;")
txtstream.WriteLine("    BACKGROUND-COLOR: navy;")
txtstream.WriteLine("    FONT-FAMILY: font-family: Cambria, serif;")
txtstream.WriteLine("    FONT-SIZE: 10px;")
txtstream.WriteLine("    text-align: left;")
txtstream.WriteLine("    white-Space: nowrap;")
txtstream.WriteLine("}")
txtstream.WriteLine("span")
txtstream.WriteLine("{")
txtstream.WriteLine("    BORDER-RIGHT: #999999 3px solid;")
txtstream.WriteLine("    PADDING-RIGHT: 3px;")
txtstream.WriteLine("    PADDING-LEFT: 3px;")
txtstream.WriteLine("    FONT-WEIGHT: Normal;")
txtstream.WriteLine("    PADDING-BOTTOM: 3px;")
txtstream.WriteLine("    COLOR: white;")
txtstream.WriteLine("    PADDING-TOP: 3px;")
txtstream.WriteLine("    BORDER-BOTTOM: #999 1px solid;")
txtstream.WriteLine("    BACKGROUND-COLOR: navy;")
txtstream.WriteLine("    FONT-FAMILY: font-family: Cambria, serif;")
txtstream.WriteLine("    FONT-SIZE: 10px;")
txtstream.WriteLine("    text-align: left;")
txtstream.WriteLine("    white-Space: nowrap;")
txtstream.WriteLine("    display:inline-block;")
txtstream.WriteLine("    width: 100%;")
txtstream.WriteLine("}")
txtstream.WriteLine("textarea")
txtstream.WriteLine("{")
txtstream.WriteLine("    BORDER-RIGHT: #999999 3px solid;")
txtstream.WriteLine("    PADDING-RIGHT: 3px;")
txtstream.WriteLine("    PADDING-LEFT: 3px;")
txtstream.WriteLine("    FONT-WEIGHT: Normal;")
```

```
txtstream.WriteLine("    PADDING-BOTTOM: 3px;")
txtstream.WriteLine("    COLOR: white;")
txtstream.WriteLine("    PADDING-TOP: 3px;")
txtstream.WriteLine("    BORDER-BOTTOM: #999 1px solid;")
txtstream.WriteLine("    BACKGROUND-COLOR: navy;")
txtstream.WriteLine("    FONT-FAMILY: font-family: Cambria, serif;")
txtstream.WriteLine("    FONT-SIZE: 10px;")
txtstream.WriteLine("    text-align: left;")
txtstream.WriteLine("    white-Space: nowrap;")
txtstream.WriteLine("    width: 100%;")
txtstream.WriteLine("}")
txtstream.WriteLine("select")
txtstream.WriteLine("{")
txtstream.WriteLine("    BORDER-RIGHT: #999999 3px solid;")
txtstream.WriteLine("    PADDING-RIGHT: 6px;")
txtstream.WriteLine("    PADDING-LEFT: 6px;")
txtstream.WriteLine("    FONT-WEIGHT: Normal;")
txtstream.WriteLine("    PADDING-BOTTOM: 6px;")
txtstream.WriteLine("    COLOR: white;")
txtstream.WriteLine("    PADDING-TOP: 6px;")
txtstream.WriteLine("    BORDER-BOTTOM: #999 1px solid;")
txtstream.WriteLine("    BACKGROUND-COLOR: navy;")
txtstream.WriteLine("    FONT-FAMILY: font-family: Cambria, serif;")
txtstream.WriteLine("    FONT-SIZE: 10px;")
txtstream.WriteLine("    text-align: left;")
txtstream.WriteLine("    white-Space: nowrap;")
txtstream.WriteLine("    width: 100%;")
txtstream.WriteLine("}")
txtstream.WriteLine("input")
txtstream.WriteLine("{")
txtstream.WriteLine("    BORDER-RIGHT: #999999 3px solid;")
txtstream.WriteLine("    PADDING-RIGHT: 3px;")
txtstream.WriteLine("    PADDING-LEFT: 3px;")
txtstream.WriteLine("    FONT-WEIGHT: Bold;")
txtstream.WriteLine("    PADDING-BOTTOM: 3px;")
txtstream.WriteLine("    COLOR: white;")
txtstream.WriteLine("    PADDING-TOP: 3px;")
txtstream.WriteLine("    BORDER-BOTTOM: #999 1px solid;")
txtstream.WriteLine("    BACKGROUND-COLOR: navy;")
txtstream.WriteLine("    FONT-FAMILY: font-family: Cambria, serif;")
```

```
txtstream.WriteLine("    FONT-SIZE: 12px;")
txtstream.WriteLine("    text-align: left;")
txtstream.WriteLine("    display:table-cell;")
txtstream.WriteLine("    white-Space: nowrap;")
txtstream.WriteLine("    width: 100%;")
txtstream.WriteLine("}")
txtstream.WriteLine("h1 {")
txtstream.WriteLine("color: antiquewhite;")
txtstream.WriteLine("text-shadow: 1px 1px 1px black;")
txtstream.WriteLine("padding: 3px;")
txtstream.WriteLine("text-align: center;")
txtstream.WriteLine("box-shadow: in2px 2px 5px rgba(0,0,0,0.5), in-2px -2px 5px rgba(255,255,255,0.5);")
txtstream.WriteLine("}")
txtstream.WriteLine("</style>")

Case "ShadowBox"

txtstream.WriteLine("<style type='text/css'>")
txtstream.WriteLine("body")
txtstream.WriteLine("{")
txtstream.WriteLine("    PADDING-RIGHT: 0px;")
txtstream.WriteLine("    PADDING-LEFT: 0px;")
txtstream.WriteLine("    PADDING-BOTTOM: 0px;")
txtstream.WriteLine("    MARGIN: 0px;")
txtstream.WriteLine("    COLOR: #333;")
txtstream.WriteLine("    PADDING-TOP: 0px;")
txtstream.WriteLine("    FONT-FAMILY: verdana, arial, helvetica, sans-serif;")
txtstream.WriteLine("}")
txtstream.WriteLine("table")
txtstream.WriteLine("{")
txtstream.WriteLine("    BORDER-RIGHT: #999999 1px solid;")
txtstream.WriteLine("    PADDING-RIGHT: 1px;")
txtstream.WriteLine("    PADDING-LEFT: 1px;")
txtstream.WriteLine("    PADDING-BOTTOM: 1px;")
txtstream.WriteLine("    LINE-HEIGHT: 8px;")
txtstream.WriteLine("    PADDING-TOP: 1px;")
txtstream.WriteLine("    BORDER-BOTTOM: #999 1px solid;")
txtstream.WriteLine("    BACKGROUND-COLOR: #eeeeee;")
```

```
                txtstream.WriteLine("
filter:progid:DXImageTransform.Microsoft.Shadow(color='silver',        Direction=135,
Strength=16)")
                txtstream.WriteLine("}")
                txtstream.WriteLine("th")
                txtstream.WriteLine("{")
                txtstream.WriteLine("   BORDER-RIGHT: #999999 3px solid;")
                txtstream.WriteLine("   PADDING-RIGHT: 6px;")
                txtstream.WriteLine("   PADDING-LEFT: 6px;")
                txtstream.WriteLine("   FONT-WEIGHT: Bold;")
                txtstream.WriteLine("   FONT-SIZE: 14px;")
                txtstream.WriteLine("   PADDING-BOTTOM: 6px;")
                txtstream.WriteLine("   COLOR: darkred;")
                txtstream.WriteLine("   LINE-HEIGHT: 14px;")
                txtstream.WriteLine("   PADDING-TOP: 6px;")
                txtstream.WriteLine("   BORDER-BOTTOM: #999 1px solid;")
                txtstream.WriteLine("   BACKGROUND-COLOR: #eeeeee;")
                txtstream.WriteLine("   FONT-FAMILY: font-family: Cambria, serif;")
                txtstream.WriteLine("   FONT-SIZE: 12px;")
                txtstream.WriteLine("   text-align: left;")
                txtstream.WriteLine("   white-Space: nowrap;")
                txtstream.WriteLine("}")
                txtstream.WriteLine(".th")
                txtstream.WriteLine("{")
                txtstream.WriteLine("   BORDER-RIGHT: #999999 2px solid;")
                txtstream.WriteLine("   PADDING-RIGHT: 6px;")
                txtstream.WriteLine("   PADDING-LEFT: 6px;")
                txtstream.WriteLine("   FONT-WEIGHT: Bold;")
                txtstream.WriteLine("   PADDING-BOTTOM: 6px;")
                txtstream.WriteLine("   COLOR: black;")
                txtstream.WriteLine("   PADDING-TOP: 6px;")
                txtstream.WriteLine("   BORDER-BOTTOM: #999 2px solid;")
                txtstream.WriteLine("   BACKGROUND-COLOR: #eeeeee;")
                txtstream.WriteLine("   FONT-FAMILY: font-family: Cambria, serif;")
                txtstream.WriteLine("   FONT-SIZE: 10px;")
                txtstream.WriteLine("   text-align: right;")
                txtstream.WriteLine("   white-Space: nowrap;")
                txtstream.WriteLine("}")
                txtstream.WriteLine("td")
                txtstream.WriteLine("{")
```

```
txtstream.WriteLine("    BORDER-RIGHT: #999999 3px solid;")
txtstream.WriteLine("    PADDING-RIGHT: 6px;")
txtstream.WriteLine("    PADDING-LEFT: 6px;")
txtstream.WriteLine("    FONT-WEIGHT: Normal;")
txtstream.WriteLine("    PADDING-BOTTOM: 6px;")
txtstream.WriteLine("    COLOR: navy;")
txtstream.WriteLine("    LINE-HEIGHT: 14px;")
txtstream.WriteLine("    PADDING-TOP: 6px;")
txtstream.WriteLine("    BORDER-BOTTOM: #999 1px solid;")
txtstream.WriteLine("    BACKGROUND-COLOR: #eeeeee;")
txtstream.WriteLine("    FONT-FAMILY: font-family: Cambria, serif;")
txtstream.WriteLine("    FONT-SIZE: 12px;")
txtstream.WriteLine("    text-align: left;")
txtstream.WriteLine("    white-Space: nowrap;")
txtstream.WriteLine("}")
txtstream.WriteLine("div")
txtstream.WriteLine("{")
txtstream.WriteLine("    BORDER-RIGHT: #999999 3px solid;")
txtstream.WriteLine("    PADDING-RIGHT: 6px;")
txtstream.WriteLine("    PADDING-LEFT: 6px;")
txtstream.WriteLine("    FONT-WEIGHT: Normal;")
txtstream.WriteLine("    PADDING-BOTTOM: 6px;")
txtstream.WriteLine("    COLOR: white;")
txtstream.WriteLine("    PADDING-TOP: 6px;")
txtstream.WriteLine("    BORDER-BOTTOM: #999 1px solid;")
txtstream.WriteLine("    BACKGROUND-COLOR: navy;")
txtstream.WriteLine("    FONT-FAMILY: font-family: Cambria, serif;")
txtstream.WriteLine("    FONT-SIZE: 10px;")
txtstream.WriteLine("    text-align: left;")
txtstream.WriteLine("    white-Space: nowrap;")
txtstream.WriteLine("}")
txtstream.WriteLine("span")
txtstream.WriteLine("{")
txtstream.WriteLine("    BORDER-RIGHT: #999999 3px solid;")
txtstream.WriteLine("    PADDING-RIGHT: 3px;")
txtstream.WriteLine("    PADDING-LEFT: 3px;")
txtstream.WriteLine("    FONT-WEIGHT: Normal;")
txtstream.WriteLine("    PADDING-BOTTOM: 3px;")
txtstream.WriteLine("    COLOR: white;")
txtstream.WriteLine("    PADDING-TOP: 3px;")
```

```
txtstream.WriteLine("    BORDER-BOTTOM: #999 1px solid;")
txtstream.WriteLine("    BACKGROUND-COLOR: navy;")
txtstream.WriteLine("    FONT-FAMILY: font-family: Cambria, serif;")
txtstream.WriteLine("    FONT-SIZE: 10px;")
txtstream.WriteLine("    text-align: left;")
txtstream.WriteLine("    white-Space: nowrap;")
txtstream.WriteLine("    display: inline-block;")
txtstream.WriteLine("    width: 100%;")
txtstream.WriteLine("}")
txtstream.WriteLine("textarea")
txtstream.WriteLine("{")
txtstream.WriteLine("    BORDER-RIGHT: #999999 3px solid;")
txtstream.WriteLine("    PADDING-RIGHT: 3px;")
txtstream.WriteLine("    PADDING-LEFT: 3px;")
txtstream.WriteLine("    FONT-WEIGHT: Normal;")
txtstream.WriteLine("    PADDING-BOTTOM: 3px;")
txtstream.WriteLine("    COLOR: white;")
txtstream.WriteLine("    PADDING-TOP: 3px;")
txtstream.WriteLine("    BORDER-BOTTOM: #999 1px solid;")
txtstream.WriteLine("    BACKGROUND-COLOR: navy;")
txtstream.WriteLine("    FONT-FAMILY: font-family: Cambria, serif;")
txtstream.WriteLine("    FONT-SIZE: 10px;")
txtstream.WriteLine("    text-align: left;")
txtstream.WriteLine("    white-Space: nowrap;")
txtstream.WriteLine("    width: 100%;")
txtstream.WriteLine("}")
txtstream.WriteLine("select")
txtstream.WriteLine("{")
txtstream.WriteLine("    BORDER-RIGHT: #999999 3px solid;")
txtstream.WriteLine("    PADDING-RIGHT: 6px;")
txtstream.WriteLine("    PADDING-LEFT: 6px;")
txtstream.WriteLine("    FONT-WEIGHT: Normal;")
txtstream.WriteLine("    PADDING-BOTTOM: 6px;")
txtstream.WriteLine("    COLOR: white;")
txtstream.WriteLine("    PADDING-TOP: 6px;")
txtstream.WriteLine("    BORDER-BOTTOM: #999 1px solid;")
txtstream.WriteLine("    BACKGROUND-COLOR: navy;")
txtstream.WriteLine("    FONT-FAMILY: font-family: Cambria, serif;")
txtstream.WriteLine("    FONT-SIZE: 10px;")
txtstream.WriteLine("    text-align: left;")
```

```
txtstream.WriteLine("   white-Space: nowrap;")
txtstream.WriteLine("   width: 100%;")
txtstream.WriteLine("}")
txtstream.WriteLine("input")
txtstream.WriteLine("{")
txtstream.WriteLine("   BORDER-RIGHT: #999999 3px solid;")
txtstream.WriteLine("   PADDING-RIGHT: 3px;")
txtstream.WriteLine("   PADDING-LEFT: 3px;")
txtstream.WriteLine("   FONT-WEIGHT: Bold;")
txtstream.WriteLine("   PADDING-BOTTOM: 3px;")
txtstream.WriteLine("   COLOR: white;")
txtstream.WriteLine("   PADDING-TOP: 3px;")
txtstream.WriteLine("   BORDER-BOTTOM: #999 1px solid;")
txtstream.WriteLine("   BACKGROUND-COLOR: navy;")
txtstream.WriteLine("   FONT-FAMILY: font-family: Cambria, serif;")
txtstream.WriteLine("   FONT-SIZE: 12px;")
txtstream.WriteLine("   text-align: left;")
txtstream.WriteLine("   display: table-cell;")
txtstream.WriteLine("   white-Space: nowrap;")
txtstream.WriteLine("   width: 100%;")
txtstream.WriteLine("}")
txtstream.WriteLine("h1 {")
txtstream.WriteLine("color: antiquewhite;")
txtstream.WriteLine("text-shadow: 1px 1px 1px black;")
txtstream.WriteLine("padding: 3px;")
txtstream.WriteLine("text-align: center;")
txtstream.WriteLine("box-shadow: in2px 2px 5px rgba(0,0,0,0.5), in-2px -2px 5px rgba(255,255,255,0.5);")
txtstream.WriteLine("}")
txtstream.WriteLine("</style>")

    Case "Customized"

txtstream.WriteLine("<style type='text/css'>")
txtstream.WriteLine("body")
txtstream.WriteLine("{")
txtstream.WriteLine("   PADDING-RIGHT: 0px;")
txtstream.WriteLine("   PADDING-LEFT: 0px;")
txtstream.WriteLine("   PADDING-BOTTOM: 0px;")
txtstream.WriteLine("   MARGIN: 0px;")
```

```
txtstream.WriteLine("    COLOR: #333;")
txtstream.WriteLine("    PADDING-TOP: 0px;")
txtstream.WriteLine("    FONT-FAMILY: verdana, arial, helvetica, sans-serif;")
txtstream.WriteLine("}")
txtstream.WriteLine("Table")
txtstream.WriteLine("{")
txtstream.WriteLine("    BORDER-RIGHT: #999999 1px solid;")
txtstream.WriteLine("    PADDING-RIGHT: 1px;")
txtstream.WriteLine("    PADDING-LEFT: 1px;")
txtstream.WriteLine("    PADDING-BOTTOM: 1px;")
txtstream.WriteLine("    LINE-HEIGHT: 8px;")
txtstream.WriteLine("    PADDING-TOP: 1px;")
txtstream.WriteLine("    BORDER-BOTTOM: #999 1px solid;")
txtstream.WriteLine("    BACKGROUND-COLOR: #eeeeee;")
txtstream.WriteLine("    filter:progid:DXImageTransform.Microsoft.Shadow(color='silver',    Direction=135, Strength=16)")
txtstream.WriteLine("}")
txtstream.WriteLine("th")
txtstream.WriteLine("{")
txtstream.WriteLine("    BORDER-RIGHT: #999999 3px solid;")
txtstream.WriteLine("    PADDING-RIGHT: 6px;")
txtstream.WriteLine("    PADDING-LEFT: 6px;")
txtstream.WriteLine("    FONT-WEIGHT: Bold;")
txtstream.WriteLine("    FONT-SIZE: 14px;")
txtstream.WriteLine("    PADDING-BOTTOM: 6px;")
txtstream.WriteLine("    COLOR: darkred;")
txtstream.WriteLine("    LINE-HEIGHT: 14px;")
txtstream.WriteLine("    PADDING-TOP: 6px;")
txtstream.WriteLine("    BORDER-BOTTOM: #999 1px solid;")
txtstream.WriteLine("    BACKGROUND-COLOR: #eeeeee;")
txtstream.WriteLine("    FONT-FAMILY: font-family: Cambria, serif;")
txtstream.WriteLine("    FONT-SIZE: 12px;")
txtstream.WriteLine("    text-align: left;")
txtstream.WriteLine("    white-Space: nowrap;")
txtstream.WriteLine("}")
txtstream.WriteLine(".th")
txtstream.WriteLine("{")
txtstream.WriteLine("    BORDER-RIGHT: #999999 2px solid;")
```

```
txtstream.WriteLine("    PADDING-RIGHT: 6px;")
txtstream.WriteLine("    PADDING-LEFT: 6px;")
txtstream.WriteLine("    FONT-WEIGHT: Bold;")
txtstream.WriteLine("    PADDING-BOTTOM: 6px;")
txtstream.WriteLine("    COLOR: black;")
txtstream.WriteLine("    PADDING-TOP: 6px;")
txtstream.WriteLine("    BORDER-BOTTOM: #999 2px solid;")
txtstream.WriteLine("    BACKGROUND-COLOR: #eeeeee;")
txtstream.WriteLine("    FONT-FAMILY: font-family: Cambria, serif;")
txtstream.WriteLine("    FONT-SIZE: 10px;")
txtstream.WriteLine("    text-align: right;")
txtstream.WriteLine("    white-Space: nowrap;")
txtstream.WriteLine("}")
txtstream.WriteLine("td")
txtstream.WriteLine("{")
txtstream.WriteLine("    BORDER-RIGHT: #999999 3px solid;")
txtstream.WriteLine("    PADDING-RIGHT: 6px;")
txtstream.WriteLine("    PADDING-LEFT: 6px;")
txtstream.WriteLine("    FONT-WEIGHT: Normal;")
txtstream.WriteLine("    PADDING-BOTTOM: 6px;")
txtstream.WriteLine("    COLOR: navy;")
txtstream.WriteLine("    LINE-HEIGHT: 14px;")
txtstream.WriteLine("    PADDING-TOP: 6px;")
txtstream.WriteLine("    BORDER-BOTTOM: #999 1px solid;")
txtstream.WriteLine("    BACKGROUND-COLOR: #eeeeee;")
txtstream.WriteLine("    FONT-FAMILY: font-family: Cambria, serif;")
txtstream.WriteLine("    FONT-SIZE: 12px;")
txtstream.WriteLine("    text-align: left;")
txtstream.WriteLine("    white-Space: nowrap;")
txtstream.WriteLine("}")
txtstream.WriteLine("div")
txtstream.WriteLine("{")
txtstream.WriteLine("    BORDER-RIGHT: #999999 3px solid;")
txtstream.WriteLine("    PADDING-RIGHT: 6px;")
txtstream.WriteLine("    PADDING-LEFT: 6px;")
txtstream.WriteLine("    FONT-WEIGHT: Normal;")
txtstream.WriteLine("    PADDING-BOTTOM: 6px;")
txtstream.WriteLine("    COLOR: white;")
txtstream.WriteLine("    PADDING-TOP: 6px;")
txtstream.WriteLine("    BORDER-BOTTOM: #999 1px solid;")
```

```
txtstream.WriteLine("    BACKGROUND-COLOR: navy;")
txtstream.WriteLine("    FONT-FAMILY: font-family: Cambria, serif;")
txtstream.WriteLine("    FONT-SIZE: 10px;")
txtstream.WriteLine("    text-align: left;")
txtstream.WriteLine("    white-Space: nowrap;")
txtstream.WriteLine("}")
txtstream.WriteLine("span")
txtstream.WriteLine("{")
txtstream.WriteLine("    BORDER-RIGHT: #999999 3px solid;")
txtstream.WriteLine("    PADDING-RIGHT: 3px;")
txtstream.WriteLine("    PADDING-LEFT: 3px;")
txtstream.WriteLine("    FONT-WEIGHT: Normal;")
txtstream.WriteLine("    PADDING-BOTTOM: 3px;")
txtstream.WriteLine("    COLOR: white;")
txtstream.WriteLine("    PADDING-TOP: 3px;")
txtstream.WriteLine("    BORDER-BOTTOM: #999 1px solid;")
txtstream.WriteLine("    BACKGROUND-COLOR: navy;")
txtstream.WriteLine("    FONT-FAMILY: font-family: Cambria, serif;")
txtstream.WriteLine("    FONT-SIZE: 10px;")
txtstream.WriteLine("    text-align: left;")
txtstream.WriteLine("    white-Space: nowrap;")
txtstream.WriteLine("    display: inline-block;")
txtstream.WriteLine("    width: 100%;")
txtstream.WriteLine("}")
txtstream.WriteLine("textarea")
txtstream.WriteLine("{")
txtstream.WriteLine("    BORDER-RIGHT: #999999 3px solid;")
txtstream.WriteLine("    PADDING-RIGHT: 3px;")
txtstream.WriteLine("    PADDING-LEFT: 3px;")
txtstream.WriteLine("    FONT-WEIGHT: Normal;")
txtstream.WriteLine("    PADDING-BOTTOM: 3px;")
txtstream.WriteLine("    COLOR: white;")
txtstream.WriteLine("    PADDING-TOP: 3px;")
txtstream.WriteLine("    BORDER-BOTTOM: #999 1px solid;")
txtstream.WriteLine("    BACKGROUND-COLOR: navy;")
txtstream.WriteLine("    FONT-FAMILY: font-family: Cambria, serif;")
txtstream.WriteLine("    FONT-SIZE: 12px;")
txtstream.WriteLine("    text-align: left;")
txtstream.WriteLine("    width: 100%;")
txtstream.WriteLine("}")
```

```
txtstream.WriteLine("select")
txtstream.WriteLine("{")
txtstream.WriteLine("   BORDER-RIGHT: #999999 1px solid;")
txtstream.WriteLine("   PADDING-RIGHT: 1px;")
txtstream.WriteLine("   PADDING-LEFT: 1px;")
txtstream.WriteLine("   FONT-WEIGHT: Normal;")
txtstream.WriteLine("   PADDING-BOTTOM: 1px;")
txtstream.WriteLine("   COLOR: white;")
txtstream.WriteLine("   PADDING-TOP: 1px;")
txtstream.WriteLine("   BORDER-BOTTOM: #999 1px solid;")
txtstream.WriteLine("   BACKGROUND-COLOR: navy;")
txtstream.WriteLine("   FONT-FAMILY: Cambria, serif;")
txtstream.WriteLine("   FONT-SIZE: 12px;")
txtstream.WriteLine("   text-align: left;")
txtstream.WriteLine("   white-Space: nowrap;")
txtstream.WriteLine("   width: 450px;")
txtstream.WriteLine("}")
txtstream.WriteLine("select1")
txtstream.WriteLine("{")
txtstream.WriteLine("   BORDER-RIGHT: #999999 1px solid;")
txtstream.WriteLine("   PADDING-RIGHT: 1px;")
txtstream.WriteLine("   PADDING-LEFT: 1px;")
txtstream.WriteLine("   FONT-WEIGHT: Normal;")
txtstream.WriteLine("   PADDING-BOTTOM: 1px;")
txtstream.WriteLine("   COLOR: white;")
txtstream.WriteLine("   PADDING-TOP: 1px;")
txtstream.WriteLine("   BORDER-BOTTOM: #999 1px solid;")
txtstream.WriteLine("   BACKGROUND-COLOR: navy;")
txtstream.WriteLine("   FONT-FAMILY: Cambria, serif;")
txtstream.WriteLine("   FONT-SIZE: 12px;")
txtstream.WriteLine("   text-align: left;")
txtstream.WriteLine("   white-Space: nowrap;")
txtstream.WriteLine("   width: 450px;")
txtstream.WriteLine("}")
txtstream.WriteLine("select2")
txtstream.WriteLine("{")
txtstream.WriteLine("   BORDER-RIGHT: #999999 1px solid;")
txtstream.WriteLine("   PADDING-RIGHT: 1px;")
txtstream.WriteLine("   PADDING-LEFT: 1px;")
txtstream.WriteLine("   FONT-WEIGHT: Normal;")
```

```
txtstream.WriteLine("    PADDING-BOTTOM: 1px;")
txtstream.WriteLine("    COLOR: white;")
txtstream.WriteLine("    PADDING-TOP: 1px;")
txtstream.WriteLine("    BORDER-BOTTOM: #999 1px solid;")
txtstream.WriteLine("    BACKGROUND-COLOR: navy;")
txtstream.WriteLine("    FONT-FAMILY: Cambria, serif;")
txtstream.WriteLine("    FONT-SIZE: 12px;")
txtstream.WriteLine("    text-align: left;")
txtstream.WriteLine("    white-Space: nowrap;")
txtstream.WriteLine("    width: 450px;")
txtstream.WriteLine("}")
txtstream.WriteLine("select3")
txtstream.WriteLine("{")
txtstream.WriteLine("    BORDER-RIGHT: #999999 1px solid;")
txtstream.WriteLine("    PADDING-RIGHT: 1px;")
txtstream.WriteLine("    PADDING-LEFT: 1px;")
txtstream.WriteLine("    FONT-WEIGHT: Normal;")
txtstream.WriteLine("    PADDING-BOTTOM: 1px;")
txtstream.WriteLine("    COLOR: white;")
txtstream.WriteLine("    PADDING-TOP: 1px;")
txtstream.WriteLine("    BORDER-BOTTOM: #999 1px solid;")
txtstream.WriteLine("    BACKGROUND-COLOR: navy;")
txtstream.WriteLine("    FONT-FAMILY: Cambria, serif;")
txtstream.WriteLine("    FONT-SIZE: 12px;")
txtstream.WriteLine("    text-align: left;")
txtstream.WriteLine("    white-Space: nowrap;")
txtstream.WriteLine("    width: 100px;")
txtstream.WriteLine("}")
txtstream.WriteLine("select4")
txtstream.WriteLine("{")
txtstream.WriteLine("    BORDER-RIGHT: #999999 1px solid;")
txtstream.WriteLine("    PADDING-RIGHT: 1px;")
txtstream.WriteLine("    PADDING-LEFT: 1px;")
txtstream.WriteLine("    FONT-WEIGHT: Normal;")
txtstream.WriteLine("    PADDING-BOTTOM: 1px;")
txtstream.WriteLine("    COLOR: white;")
txtstream.WriteLine("    PADDING-TOP: 1px;")
txtstream.WriteLine("    BORDER-BOTTOM: #999 1px solid;")
txtstream.WriteLine("    BACKGROUND-COLOR: navy;")
txtstream.WriteLine("    FONT-FAMILY: Cambria, serif;")
```

```
txtstream.WriteLine("    FONT-SIZE: 12px;")
txtstream.WriteLine("    text-align: left;")
txtstream.WriteLine("    white-Space: nowrap;")
txtstream.WriteLine("    width: 254px;")
txtstream.WriteLine("}")
txtstream.WriteLine("input")
txtstream.WriteLine("{")
txtstream.WriteLine("    BORDER-RIGHT: #999999 3px solid;")
txtstream.WriteLine("    PADDING-RIGHT: 3px;")
txtstream.WriteLine("    PADDING-LEFT: 3px;")
txtstream.WriteLine("    FONT-WEIGHT: Bold;")
txtstream.WriteLine("    PADDING-BOTTOM: 3px;")
txtstream.WriteLine("    COLOR: white;")
txtstream.WriteLine("    PADDING-TOP: 3px;")
txtstream.WriteLine("    BORDER-BOTTOM: #999 1px solid;")
txtstream.WriteLine("    BACKGROUND-COLOR: navy;")
txtstream.WriteLine("    FONT-FAMILY: font-family: Cambria, serif;")
txtstream.WriteLine("    FONT-SIZE: 12px;")
txtstream.WriteLine("    text-align: left;")
txtstream.WriteLine("    display: table-cell;")
txtstream.WriteLine("    white-Space: nowrap;")
txtstream.WriteLine("    width: 100%;")
txtstream.WriteLine("}")
txtstream.WriteLine("</style>")

    End Select

End Sub

</script>

</body>
</html>
```

Above this line is where it ends.

Merry Christmas!

www.ingramcontent.com/pod-product-compliance
Lightning Source LLC
Chambersburg PA
CBHW071253050326
40690CB00011B/2379